An Evangelical's Guidebook

to the Holy Land

AN EVANGELICAL'S GUIDEBOOK TO THE HOLY LAND

WAYNE DEHONEY

BROADMAN PRESS
Nashville, Tennessee

ISBN: 0-8054-5701-01
4257-01

Black and white photographs by Wayne Dehoney
Color photographs by W. Murray Severance, courtesy of Broadman Films.

Library of Congress Catalog Card Number: 73-85698
Dewey Decimal Classification: 915-69
Printed in the United States of America

Dedication

To my dear friends, the Arab and Israeli guides who have so freely shared their knowledge and insights of the Holy Land through the years, and to the staff of the St. George Hotel in East Jerusalem, whose hospitality has made for me a "home away from home" on so many occasions

Contents

Introduction

Time has not dimmed the magnetic attraction of the Holy Land as visitors stream into modern-day Israel in greater numbers than ever!

What is the continuing appeal of this tiny piece of arid geography, tucked in an out-of-the-way corner of the earth along the eastern shore of the Mediterranean? This remarkable land has cradled the faith of three major world religions, Judaism, the Muslim religion, and Christianity.

To the Jew, this is the Holy Land of Promise! Four thousand years ago Abraham at the command of the living God left Ur of Chaldees and made his way into this Land of Promise. Here the patriarchs Isaac and Jacob were born. Here Joshua marched with the children of Israel to recapture the land. Here the judges Samson, Samuel, and others ruled the people. Here David was anointed king, Solomon built the first Temple, and the golden age of Judaism flourished. Here the prophets Isaiah, Jeremiah, Amos and others thundered forth their message.

This is the Promised Land of the Jew. Ever since the destruction of Jerusalem in A.D. 70 and the dispersion of the Jews, devout Jewish pilgrims have returned to this land to dream and pray for the coming of a messiah, the rebuilding of the Temple, and the restoration of their kingdom.

This is also a Holy Land to the vast Arab world of the Middle East. Muslim in faith, the Arabs consider Jerusalem and the Temple area second only to Mecca in sacred significance. They believe that the prophet Muhammad ascended from earth in the Temple area of Jerusalem and made a journey to heaven from whence he returned to earth to die at Medina.

This land also has holy significance to those of us who claim Jesus Christ as the Savior. For here Christ was born of Mary in Bethlehem. Here on this tiny bit of earth crust God was in Christ, walking, teaching, dwelling among us and making his full revelation known to man. It was here that he died on the cross for our sins and rose the third day from the dead, the living Savior and the Lord of all life.

A visit to the Holy Land is more than a tour of a faraway land to view the sights of an ancient culture and a strange people. It is a pilgrimage and spiritual quest. As you visit the actual sites of the historical events, the Bible comes alive. As you follow in the footsteps of Jesus around the Sea of Galilee, to Bethany, into the garden of Gethsemane, and to Calvary, you feel the presence and the power of the living Lord in a way never before known.

I recall one Sunday on the mountainous windswept fortress of Masada overlooking the Dead Sea. We had gathered for a worship service amid the ruins of a first-century Jewish synagogue. In the group was a young man who claimed to be an atheist. He later confessed

The rock-hewn Garden Tomb, traditional site of Christ's burial, located north of the walled city of Jerusalem

his purpose in making the trip. He accompanied his parents to purchase illegal drugs in the Middle East and smuggle them into the United States under the security of a Christian tour group. As I preached of how God had revealed himself in many ways, through nature, the prophets, and finally here in this land through his Son Jesus Christ, the living Lord spoke to the heart of this young man. At that moment and place he discovered Jesus Christ as his personal Lord and Savior. Again and again I have seen such miracles happen as Christ has become intimately real and personal to many people as we have traveled this Holy Land.

Always there are those mountaintop spiritual experiences: the sunrise resurrection service in the garden tomb; a prayer meeting in the garden of Gethsemane; the reading of Scripture on the rooftop of the house of Simon the Tanner in Joppa where Peter received his vision to preach the gospel to the Gentiles; the singing of a Christmas carol in Bethlehem at the site where Christ was born; the soloist singing, "Fill my cup, Lord," at Jacob's well where Jesus talked to the Samaritan woman about the water of life!

In this guidebook I have presented the essential biblical and historical information concerning the principal sites that you will visit. I have interwoven personal impressions and spiritual insights accumulated through many years of conducting study-travel seminars to the Holy Land.

I have not dealt with the finer points of archaeology

nor sought to resolve the debates concerning the authenticity of certain sites. For example, there is the question of the authentic site of the burial of our Lord, in the Church of the Holy Sepulchre or in the garden tomb? To me this question is overshadowed by the supremely significant fact that, at one place or the other, or yet still another undiscovered spot nearby there is an empty tomb! For we know from personal experience with this living Lord: "He is not here. He is risen and is alive forevermore!" As the site becomes symbolic of the greater truth, a sincere believer at *either place* can experience the presence and power of the living Lord and reaffirm the reality of the resurrection!

At times I will cite the lack of archaeological evidence and identify a site as "traditional." Again, the fact that archaeology does not authenticate the exact location of a certain event does not in any way detract from the reality of that event which did occur! As the traditional site commemorates that event, the event becomes a living reality to those who look through the eyes of the Spirit.

So I invite you to take your Bible in hand and go with me on this pilgrimage. Let your heart be open and your spirit sensitive. May the sites and recollections of an ancient yesterday be the means whereby the living Lord makes himself known to you today.

1

Arrival and Briefing

You have arrived in Jerusalem.

You are a bit sleepy from the "short" night. Leaving the States by jet in the late evening, you had leisurely finished your dinner aloft and just dozed off to sleep when the stewardess was back again with your breakfast and instructed you to set your watch forward from 1:00 A.M. to 7:00 A.M. European time. While you were drinking your coffee, you saw an unforgettable sunrise as your plane skimmed at thirty thousand feet over what seemed to be an endless ocean of billowing cotton.

After a seven-hour flight, you landed in Europe, and then took off for Israel, again setting your watch forward one more hour. When you landed at Lod Airport just east of Tel Aviv and saw the skyscrapers, jet planes, and four-lane expressways, you wondered, can this be the ancient land of the Bible? But after an hour's bus ride twisting up through the hills, you rounded a curve and saw *Jerusalem!* There were the massive stone walls and flat stone houses and men in strange dress riding donkeys in the streets—and you knew your dream of a lifetime had come true. You were in the Holy Land!

Now you are checked into your hotel room. Looking out your window toward the Old City, the lengthened shadows tell you that night and bedtime are drawing near. But your "body clock" says it is not yet noontime on your schedule. It is too late to go sightseeing. So why not spend this evening becoming familiar with the background of this land.

You know your Bible reasonably well. But in the next few days you will encounter many nonbiblical references—words and names. Many people have come and gone in this land since the New Testament era and they have left their mark. A brief outline of post-biblical history, personalities, and peoples will give you a frame of reference for many things you will see in the exciting days ahead.

The Romans

The period 46 B.C. to A.D. 180 marked the zenith of Rome's glory. It was a time of peace throughout the Empire, of great cultural expansion, and the perfection of the political organization. The Empire extended from the Atlantic to the Euphrates and from the North Sea to the African desert. The population of the Empire in the days of Jesus has been estimated at two hundred ten million people.

In Palestine, proud Jews, chafing under Roman occupation, were in a constant state of unrest. Acts of rebellion occurred with increasing frequency until Rome's patience was exhausted. The Roman armies swept through Palestine, leveling Jerusalem under General Titus in A.D. 70, slaughtering an estimated one million people, and dispersing the Jews. Christians were identified as a sect of Judaism and suffered in the persecutions that followed.

The emperors of the New Testament era were:

Augustus Caesar, 31 B.C. to A.D. 14 (Christ born)
Tiberius Caesar, A.D. 14-37 (Christ crucified)
Caligula, A.D. 37-41
Claudius, A.D. 41-54
Nero, A.D. 54-68 (Severe persecution of Christians, execution of Paul)
Galba, A.D. 68-69
Otho and Vitellius, A.D. 69
Vespasian, A.D. 69-79 (Jerusalem destroyed)
Titus, A.D. 79-81
Domitian, A.D. 81-96 (Severe persecution of Christians, banishment of John)

Thereafter in the next two centuries a series of emperors ascended to the throne in Rome. There were varying degress of toleration and persecution of Christians. During this period many pagan temples were erected on traditional Christian sites in the Holy Land in an effort to stamp out all remembrance of Christianity among the local peoples. Then Constantine became emperor (A.D. 306-337).

The reign of Constantine marked a turning point in history. While engaged in warfare with competitors to establish himself as emperior, on the eve of the Battle of Milvian Bridge just outside Rome on October 27, 312, Constantine saw a vision of the cross in the sky. Above the cross were the words, "In this sign, conquer." Constantine interpreted this vision as a divine

The Damascus Gate is a major entrance to the old city of Jerusalem.

The Ecce Homo Arch in Jerusalem

The hills outside of "The Holy City"

The Garden Tomb, traditional site of Jesus' entombment

manifestation. He accepted the Christian faith, raised a banner emblazoned with a cross, and won the battle!

With his victory and conversion, Constantine became a zealous advocate of the Christian faith. Among his many official acts that furthered Christianity were:

—The Edict of Toleration. He granted Christians and all others full religious freedom and liberty. This was the first edict of its kind in history.

—He assisted in the building of churches. His mother, Queen Helena, made a pilgrimage to the Holy Land, discovered many sites of Christian significance, and erected churches on them. (We call these Constantinian *basilicas* or churches.)

—He moved the capital of the Empire from Rome to Byzantium, called it Constantinople (modern-day Istanbul), and developed it as the capital of the Byzantine Empire. We refer to the next few centuries as the Byzantine Era, and the churches built in this era as Byzantine churches.

—He commissioned the copying of the Holy Scripture and many editions of the Bible.

—He established Sunday as the Christian's day of assembly, and an official day of rest.

—He set into practice Christianity as the state religion of the Roman Empire, later an official edict under Theodosius (A.D. 378-395).

In A.D. 395 the Empire divided politically, with Constantinople as the Eastern capital and Rome as the Western capital. The Western Empire fell in A.D. 476 at the hands of the barbarians—the Goths, Vandals,

A Muslim minaret or tower adjacent to the Temple area in Jerusalem

and Huns. Europe was plunged into the Dark Ages. However, the Eastern Empire and Constantinople continued to flourish for a millennium before falling to the Turks in A.D. 1453.

The division of the Roman Empire politically resulted also in a division of the Christian churches ecclesiastically. A system of bishoprics had developed, with clearly defined geographical areas. Five great centers of Christian influence evolved. Of these, Antioch, Jerusalem, and Alexandria gradually acknowledged the leadership of Constantinople while Rome stood alone. In the centuries to follow, Rome was to become the dominant Christian influence in Western Europe and Constantinople in Eastern Europe and Asia.

This period was characterized by a constant bitter power struggle between the Patriarch of Constantinople and the Bishop of Rome. Edicts excommunicating each other were frequent. Rival church councils were held; in Constantinople with Greek as the official language and in Rome with Latin the official language.

In A.D. 1054 the official break came between the East and the West. The Eastern (or Greek) Orthodox branch of Christianity separated from the Roman (or Latin) Church. Among the issues that brought about the schism were that the Eastern Church refused to acknowledge the Pope in Rome as Lord of the whole Church, rejected the images in the Roman church as tending to idolatry (pictures or icons were allowed), insisted on baptism by immersion (not sprinkling), and permitted the priests to marry.

Today, throughout the Holy Land, you will see the abiding influence of these two branches of Christianity, the *Roman Catholic Church* and the *Eastern Orthodox Church* (and various national branches of this Eastern Church—Syrian, Armenian, Russian Orthodox, etc.).

The Arabs and the Muslim Religion

The Arabs are half brothers to the Jews, with Abraham as their father, but claiming to be descendants of Ishmael rather than Isaac. The Arabs are universally Muslim in their faith (Muslim is the Arabic for *Moslem.*), and acknowledge Muhammad as their prophet.

Muhammad was born A.D. 570 in Mecca (to the east of modern-day Israel in Arabia). He had frequent contact with Christianity and Judaism and the idolatrous paganism of the Arabs. At forty years of age (in A.D. 610) Muhammad declared himself to be a prophet sent from God. Failing to gain a following in Mecca, he fled to Medina in A.D. 622. Accepted there as a religious and military leader, Muhammad organized an army of zealous religious warriors and launched a holy conquest. In A.D. 630 he captured Mecca and destroyed 360 idols in the city. He died in A.D. 632. In Istanbul today, his hand, portions of fingernails, hair, and his sword are displayed as sacred relics.

The Muslim religion spread with the Arab military conquest of the Near East. In A.D. 634 the Arabs took Syria; 637, Jerusalem; 638, Egypt; 640, Persia. In ten years the Arabs had taken all of the Middle East.

Thus this land that cradled our faith, where Christ

An Arab Christian of Bethlehem

was born and where Constantine established the great Christian Byzantine Empire that for all practical purposes made this land solidly "Christian" until the seventh century—this land fell to the Muslims! How could such a "Christian" empire be turned into a Muslim world in one generation and remain so for thirteen centuries to this very day?

Many explanations can be offered. One of the simplest is that the church itself had become weakened and paganized. A system of Mariolatry and the worship of the saints had developed. Images, relics, and saints had become a part of the Christian practice. The Muslim religion was a revolt against this idolatry and against a degenerate and corrupt church.

The new religion of Muhammad brought other evils to replace the perversions of Christianity. It was a religion of hate, propagated by the sword, and approving slavery, polygamy, and the degradation of womanhood.

It acknowledged Jesus only as a minor prophet, with Muhammad as the final revelation of God and replaced the Bible with the Koran as the word of God.

In the next century the tidal wave of fanatical Arab Muslim soldiers moved westward and threatened Europe. In A.D. 732 in France, at the Battle of Tours, Charles Martel and his armies defeated the Muslim army and saved Europe from Islam.

The Arabs dominated the Near East in the period of A.D. 622-1058. Then the Turks (who also were Muslim by faith) came into ascendancy to rule this Eastern Empire. When Constantinople fell to the Turks in A.D. 1453, again Europe was threatened with a second Muslim invasion. But the tide was stemmed in the Battle of Vienna in A.D. 1683 by the armies led by John Sovieski.

Today in the Holy Land you see the continuing influence of the Muslim religion through the Arabs and the Turks.

The Crusades

There was yet another stream of invaders who left their mark on this land. Frequently the ruins of a Crusader church or fortress will be pointed out to you. There was a brief period of less than two hundred years when the Christians of Europe rallied armies to march into Palestine in an effort to recapture the holy places from the Muslims. In all there were seven distinct Crusades; the first of which succeeded in capturing Jerusalem (A.D. 1095-1099) and the last, a

kings on the flagstones in the Pave-
t area are believed to have been used
Roman soldiers for their games.

At Caesarea a bastion wall and moat built by French Crusaders in A.D. 1251.

aesarea a statue of Zeus dating back
he New Testament era

Mosaic of loaves and fishes at Tabtha, traditional site of Christ's feeding the five thousand

faltering effort to wrest the land from the hand of the Saracens (1270-1272).

Although the Crusades were only partially successful in recapturing portions of the Holy Land and held these spots for only a limited time, nevertheless they influenced the destiny of Europe. The Crusades stalled the westward advance of the Turks and probably saved Europe from Turkish domination and the Muslim religion!

Today

Yet another stream of influence is being brought to bear on the Holy Land today. In 1948, the nation of Israel, out of existence for nineteen centuries, again became a political reality. Never before in human history has a nation died as a political entity, to be revived again centuries later.

Many Bible students see in this modern miracle a fulfillment of prophecy! For the first time since A.D. 70 the Jews have a national homeland, Israel is a recognized political entity, and the greater portion of the geography of biblical Palestine including all the city of Jerusalem and the Temple area, is occupied by this Jewish state!

You will find it quite fascinating to see how all these postbiblical streams of influence come to bear on a particular biblical site. For example, when you go to Bethlehem (suggested for your second day) and visit the Church of the Nativity, you will find that

—A very early *tradition* places Christ's birth in this cave in Bethlehem.

—In the time of *Hadrian* (second century A.D.) a site of pagan worship was established here to discourage Christian worship.

—In A.D. 330 *Queen Helena* declared this the authentic site of the birth of Christ and a *Constantinian church* was erected.

—*Justinian* (sixth century A.D.) during the zenith of the *Byzantine era* rebuilt and enlarged the edifice.

—Mosaics were applied to the walls of the church by artisans during the *Crusader* occupation (eleventh century A.D.).

—During the *Turkish* occupation (sixteenth century A.D.) *Muslim troops* desecrated the site by stabling horses in the church. Later the arched entranceway was partially blocked in to keep out animals so that today you must stoop to enter through the tiny doorway.

—Upon entry you find three different church groups claiming rights to various areas of the church, *Roman Catholic, Greek Orthodox,* and *Armenian Orthodox.*

So as you visit the Church of the Nativity in Bethlehem you see the material evidence of many centuries of influence in the physical situation itself. But you are even more aware of the unseen spiritual presence of millions of devout pilgrims who have come from the far corners of the earth over a period of nearly two millennias to celebrate again that momentous night in human history when the angel band announced to shepherds in the nearby fields the good news, "Unto you is born a Saviour which is Christ the Lord."

2

Oh, What a Beautiful City!

Your first morning in the Holy Land! At daybreak you are awakened by a piercing wail! Standing at the window you discover that the singsong cry comes from the top of a tower or *minaret* three blocks away. It is the voice of the *muzzim,* the Muslim preacher. In days past he walked the turret of the minaret calling with a strong voice for the faithful to come to prayer. But this morning an amplified tape recording blasts his cry to the sleeping city.

If you could be at the mosque at this moment, you would see the devout Muslim unroll his prayer rug, pour water from an aluminum teakettle to wash his hands, feet, face, ears, and mouth in a ritual of purification, then kneel and bow prostrate toward Mecca beginning the first of five periods of prayer for the day. Thus begins your first day in the new and exciting land.

Later in the dining room, you become acquainted with a most un-American institution, the continental breakfast—no eggs, bacon, or corn flakes—just coffee, hard rolls, butter, and orange marmalade!

Now you are ready for your tour! Your itinerary is planned so that you may lodge in Jerusalem. Excellent roads and the proximity of the significant sites enable you to loop out of Jerusalem in different directions,

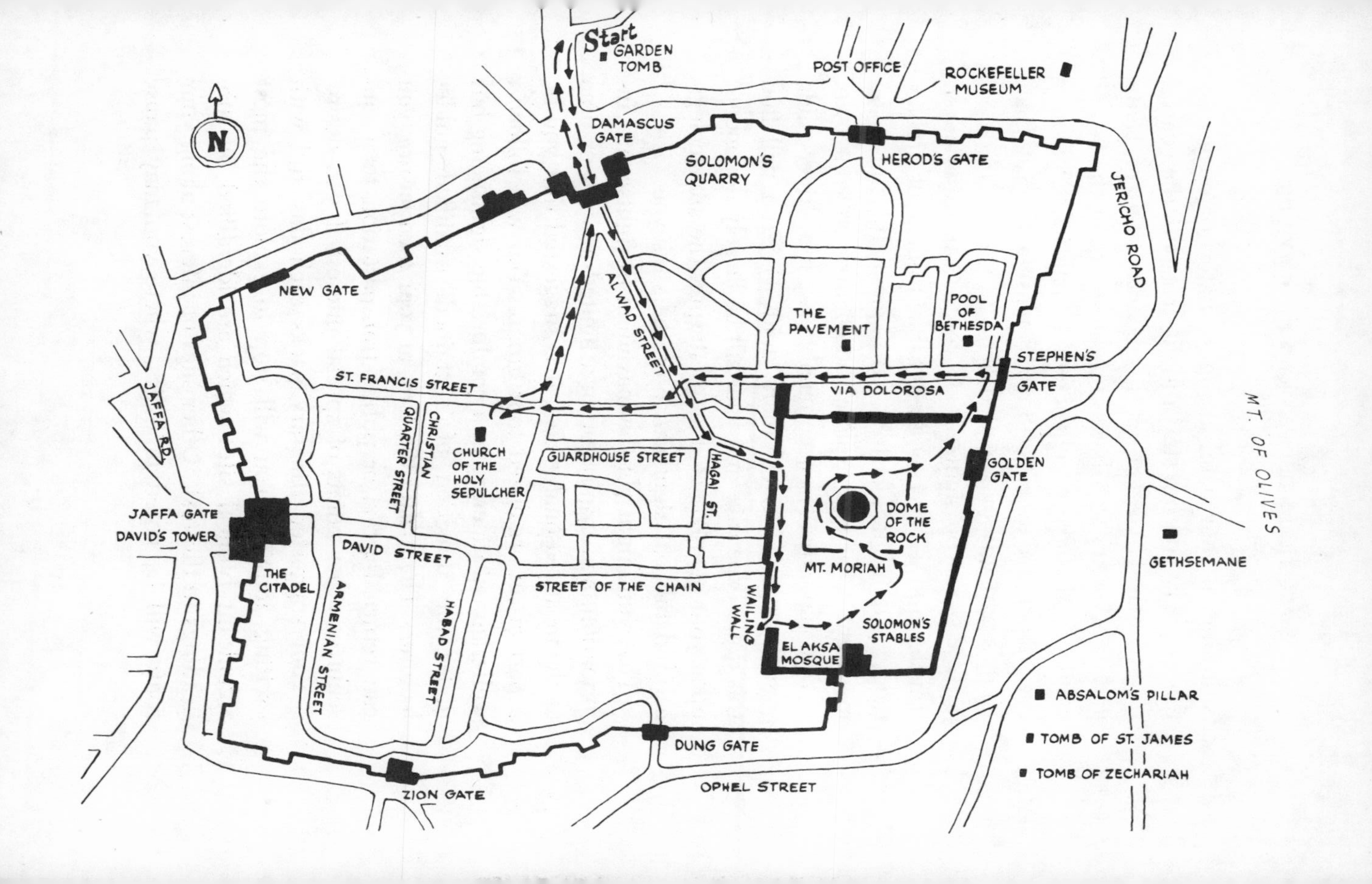
Start
GARDEN TOMB
POST OFFICE
ROCKEFELLER MUSEUM
N
DAMASCUS GATE
SOLOMON'S QUARRY
HEROD'S GATE
JERICHO ROAD
NEW GATE
AL WAD STREET
THE PAVEMENT
POOL OF BETHESDA
STEPHEN'S GATE
ST. FRANCIS STREET
VIA DOLOROSA
MT. OF OLIVES
JAFFA RD.
CHRISTIAN QUARTER STREET
CHURCH OF THE HOLY SEPULCHER
GUARDHOUSE STREET
HAGAI ST.
GOLDEN GATE
DOME OF THE ROCK
JAFFA GATE
DAVID'S TOWER
DAVID STREET
MT. MORIAH
GETHSEMANE
THE CITADEL
STREET OF THE CHAIN
WAILING WALL
SOLOMON'S STABLES
ARMENIAN STREET
HABAD STREET
EL AKSA MOSQUE
ABSALOM'S PILLAR
TOMB OF ST. JAMES
DUNG GATE
TOMB OF ZECHARIAH
ZION GATE
OPHEL STREET

returning to your hotel at night. Later, or on an extended visit, you can stay a night or two in the coastal resort area of Askelon, or the modern cities of Haifa and Tel Aviv or at Tiberias on the shores of the Sea of Galilee. All have excellent hotel facilities. You may even fly down over the Sinai Peninsula to visit Elat, Israel's port city on the Red Sea.

How shall you sightsee? If you are an experienced traveler and a very knowledgeable student of archaeology and biblical history, with plenty of time, you may rent a car and explore the country on your own.

You may engage an automobile with a driver-guide (usually more "driver" than "guide"!). You will find this quite expensive and you will be largely dependent upon your own knowledge to interpret the archaeological and biblical significance of the sites you visit.

That you might get the maximum in sightseeing, information, and inspiration in a limited amount of time at the most reasonable cost, it is suggested that you be a part of an organized tour group. You will follow a well-planned itinerary in a comfortable sightseeing bus under the direction of a trained, qualified guide-lecturer. Then, after the tour, at your own leisure, you can return by taxi or public transportation to a museum or other points of special interest if you desire.

Your suggested itinerary packs each day full with exciting activity. You will stop to explore the most significant biblical sites which are identified by subheadings in the text. Other sites of interest along your route will be noted in italics, where you may pause

; Muslim tower, called el Madrasa el-liya, now stands on the remnants of the rress of Antonio.

Remnants of the Tower of Antonio, named by Herod in honor of Mark Antony

Pavement in the Fortress of Antonio, ere Jesus was judged by Pilate

A modern mosaic in the Pavement area of the Fortress of Antonio

only long enough to "shoot a picture" and then go on.

Today you take a walking tour of the Old City of Jerusalem. Once divided between Israel and Jordan, the Six Day War of 1967 unified Jerusalem under Israeli control. The present massive walls were rebuilt in A.D. 1514 by the Turks under Suleiman the Magnificent and only in part follow the lines of the city walls of Jesus' day. There are eight gates in the two-and-a-half miles of wall that circle the city.

Gordon's Calvary and the Garden Tomb

About three blocks northeast of Herod's Gate is Gordon's Calvary and the garden tomb, a traditional site of the crucifixion and burial of our Lord (Luke 23; Matt. 27; Mark 15; John 19).

The exact site of Christ's crucifixion is unknown. It was called "Golgotha" meaning literally "the skull" (Luke 23:23), near a highway (Matt. 27:39), "without the gate" (Heb. 13:12). In recent years, Gordon's Calvary has become memorialized as the location of the crucifixion, along with a garden tomb nearby as the site of the Lord's burial.

Gordon's Calvary is named after the noted British general, Charles George "Chinese" Gordon. About a century ago, as General Gordon was walking atop the wall of Jerusalem, he pointed to this hill and remarked to a friend, "That looks just like Calvary." In the rocky limestone knoll you quite readily see the resemblance of a skull, two eyes, a crooked nose, a distorted mouth. A few years earlier, in 1849, a German, Otto Thebius, had also observed the similarity and identified the site as Calvary. But it remained for General Gordon to popularize the site. While we have no archaeological evidence to validate this spot as Calvary, from ancient times it has had the appearance of a skull, and is clearly outside the wall of the Old City.

After General Gordon had called attention to the rocky hill, excavations were conducted along the base of the cliff. A garden was discovered and in it an empty tomb, identified as possibly the unused sepulcher in the private garden of Joseph of Arimathea in which Christ was buried (John 19:38-42). The tomb is shaped somewhat like a bathtub. It apparently was lengthened approximately a foot suggesting that the tomb was altered to accommodate a larger person than originally planned. And was not Christ buried in a tomb not his own, but borrowed?

Countless thousands have come to this garden tomb with a firm conviction that this is of a certainty the tomb in which Christ was buried. The tomb in the garden, free from ecclesiastical trappings, is conducive to worship according to evangelical tradition. It is typical of the tombs of Jesus' day. Certainly if this is not the actual tomb, we know there is a tomb somewhere very near this spot where our Lord was buried. And like this tomb, his was an empty tomb, "For he is not here, but he is risen and alive forevermore."

Damascus Gate

From the garden tomb you walk to the Damascus Gate. Three hundred feet to the left of the gate at the base of the wall is the entrance to a huge cave and underground quarry. Legend identifies this cave with Zedekiah, the last king of Judah. Supposedly the cave extends all the way to the plains of Jericho and through it Zedekiah fled to safety when Jerusalem was invaded by Nebuchadnezzar (586 B.C., 2 Kings 25). The huge cavern is approximately 350 feet across and runs back 250 yards through the bedrock under the *Bezeth,* a section of Jerusalem.

This cave is popularly referred to as *Solomon's Quary.* It was discovered a century ago by an Englishman, wandering outside Jerusalem's city wall when his dog disappeared down a hole and later reappeared elsewhere. Authorities investigating the cave then identified it as the "royal caverns" referred to by the Jewish historian Josephus. This underground quarry probably supplied stone for Herod's temple and quite possibly the stone for Solomon's Temple.

First Kings 6:7 indicates that never was the "noise of a hammer or chisel heard" in the construction of Solomon's Temple. It is believed that the stone was quarried, shaped and fitted in this cave below ground. Thus the noise of the workmen was muffled and not heard in the temple area above. The stone is snow-white when freshly quarried and turns ivory with the exposure to the elements. Freemasons held early meetings in this quarry and the walls are marked by

The Garden of Gethsemane with the "Golden Gate" in the background

The Tower of David at Jerusalem

The traditional site of Jesus' baptism in the Jordan River

Another angle of the Jordan River

various symbols of the order.

You enter the old city through the main northern gate, the Damascus Gate, or "gate of the pillar." In Roman days this gate marked the beginning of a columned way into the city. One of the pillars still stands inside the gate. From this gate the road leads north to Damascus. The gate is an excellent example of the ornate Mameluke workmanship of the earlier Turkish era.

From the Damascus Gate you go through the *bazaar section* of the Muslim quarters to the Temple area.

The Temple Area

The Temple area is on the highest point of Mt. Moriah. A Muslim mosque, the Dome of the Rock, occupies the center, and the Mosque of El Aksa, the southern area. The area is surrounded by arched porticos, fountains for ablution, and the buildings of Muslim schools and monasteries.

This is an authentic site where the three successive Jewish temples once stood. It is believed that here Abraham brought Isaac to be offered (Gen. 22:1-14). This was the Jebusite threshing floor that David bought from Ornan and here erected an altar (1 Chron. 21:15-28). Here Solomon built his Temple in 950 B.C. (2 Kings 25:8-21). After the captivity, the Temple of the Restoration was built in 520 B.C.

Destroyed a second time, the Temple was rebuilt by Herod the Great (beginning about 20 B.C.) on a grander and more magnificent style. Herod's Temple was built of snow-white limestone and the east wall was covered with gold. As the sun rose over the Mount of Olives, it reflected in splendor on the gold and white. This prompted an ancient writer to declare: "You have never seen a great city if you have not seen Jerusalem—and you have never seen a great building if you have not seen the Temple built by Herod!"

From the Mount of Olives Jesus looked across the Kidron Valley upon Herod's Temple in all its splendor, weeping over the forthcoming destruction of the city —when not one stone of this magnificent building would be left upon the other.

In A.D. 70 his prophecy came to pass! The Jews revolted against the Roman army of occupation when the emperor ordered that his statue be erected in this Temple area. The Roman general Vespasian marched against Palestine in A.D. 66. But before he arrived in Jerusalem (while still at Caesarea) he was crowned emperor and returned to Rome.

His son, Titus, took over the campaign and marched on Jerusalem. With his armies encamped on Mt. Scopus (to the north) he besieged the city. He found it strongly defended with a series of three walls on the north side and high walls and steep hills on the other three sides. With great difficulty, Titus finally breached the first wall, the second wall, and broke through into the city at the site of the Temple.

In A.D. 70 the city fell. Titus burned the Temple, tearing it down completely, stone by stone, and leveling the area. Titus also destroyed the other magnificent

A striking example of Muslim architecture—with its geometric motif, inlaid marble, and glazed tile—is the Dome of the Rock.

buildings constructed by Herod and left only three towers standing near the Joppa Gate. This location is now called the *Citadel*, and the lower courses of these towers date back to the Herodian period. Titus did not completely destroy the western wall of the Temple area and the Herodian stone base of that wall is the location of the *Wailing Wall* today.

On the Temple site the Emperor Hadrian built a pagan temple. In A.D. 320 the Byzantines captured the city. They destroyed the pagan temple but neglected the immediate Temple area. Nearby, however, the Byzantines erected the Church of St. Mary.

The Dome of the Rock

In A.D. 637 the Arabs captured the city. In 691 Caliph Abd-el-Malik built this mosque, one of the finest examples of Muslim architecture anywhere in the world. He used materials from Christian churches and from other nearby buildings in the construction. In 1099 the Crusaders conquered the city and transformed the mosque into a Christian church. Then again, in 1187 the Muslim Saladin recaptured the city and the church was converted back into a mosque. This area is a most holy place for the Muslim world, second only to Mecca. Descendants of Abraham, the Muslims believe that it was Ishmael, not Isaac, who was tied on this spot to be offered to God.

Inside the Dome of the Rock is the huge outcropping of stone (2 Chron. 3:1). This limestone formation fifty feet by thirty feet, purchased by David for six hundred shekels of gold (2 Sam. 24:18-25) was the altar of sacrifice in the Temple. In the rock you see the courses or channels that carried off the water and the blood of the sacrifices. A large hole in the middle of the altar allowed the blood to run down into a cave beneath and on out through an aqueduct into the Brook Kidron. Various traditions claim that in this cave David, Solomon, the prophet Muhammad, Elisha, and Elijah came at some time to pray.

It was here, in this area where the Dome of the Rock now stands, that Jesus was found at twelve years of age teaching the elders. It was from this area immediately surrounding this rock that Jesus drove out the money changers. The actual Temple itself extended to the west of the rock and the rock was surrounded by columns.

Outside, in the court of the Gentiles, a warning was posted, "Death to the Gentile that enters into the columned area." The holy of holies itself was somewhere outside this present mosque. Once a year the priest went into the holy of holies while the people assembled inside this columned area around the rock. At the death of the Lord, the veil of silk in front of the holy of holies was rent in two.

Mosque El Aksa

About a hundred yards from the Dome of the Rock is the silver-topped mosque of El Aksa, called the "distant" mosque (the most distant spot to which

Muhammad traveled from his birthplace in Mecca). Muslims believe it was from this spot that Muhammad ascended into heaven on his white steed *al-Buraq* (as recorded in the Koran) and then descended from heaven to Medina where he was buried. Medina is to the east in Arabia.

When the Crusaders took Jerusalem in the twelfth century, this mosque was used as a residence for the Latin kings. And here was founded the Templar Order. The mosque was damaged by an earthquake in 1927 and rebuilt in 1936. In the present-day mosque is a sixth century A.D. window and some very old columns.

In these two structures you observe that Arabic designs are always geometrical. Muslim law forbids the reproduction in art form of any living object lest the people be tempted to idolatry.

Solomon's Stables

In the southeastern area of the Temple courtyard, under the pavement, are Solomon's Stables. Actually the stables you now see were built by Herod the Great in about 40 B.C. At that time there were a thousand columns or arches in these stables, and the stables were at ground level.

The debris of human occupation has filled up the area to a depth in excess of forty feet so that the stables are now far below ground level. In the fourteenth century A.D. the arches were walled in to make cisterns for water storage. A hole was cut in the arched roof above the stables to receive the water. Today there are only eighty of the open arches or columns left, the rest having been converted into cisterns. Excavations have revealed that twenty-five feet on below Herod's stables were Solomon's stables.

The southeast corner of the Temple area rises high over the Kidron Valley. This is the *pinnacle of the Temple* referred to in the second temptation of Jesus (Matt. 4:5).

The Wailing Wall

At the southeastern corner, outside the Temple area is the Wailing Wall, a portion of the remains of the construction of Herod's day. For centuries Jewish pilgrims have stood at the wall, mourning the destruction of the Temple and chanting the lamentations of Jeremiah as they have prayed for the rebuilding of a new temple. To give special efficacy to their petitions, letters and prayers to God are inserted in the cracks between the huge stones. Some believe the dew which nightly covers the stones represents the tears the wall itself sheds as it weeps over the exiled people of Israel. The wall stands as a symbol to the Jews of the faithfulness of God to his word and his promise to them of the restoration of the temple and the coming of a messiah.

St. Stephen's Gate

North of the Temple area in the eastern wall is St. Stephen's Gate (or Lion's Gate). The present wall and gate were constructed by the Turks in the Sixteenth Century A.D. on the foundations of the old Herodian wall. The wall contains some salvaged pieces of Herodian stone. The lions are the emblem of the Turkish sultan and warrior, *Baybars.* According to tradition, Stephen was brought out through this gate to be stoned while the young rabbi Saul held his garments (Acts 7:58 to 8:2). This was also called the "sheep" gate, site of the ancient sheep market which is still conducted by this gate every Friday morning.

Church of St. Anne

Fifty yards inside St. Stephen's Gate is the Church of St. Anne. A Byzantine church was first constructed on this spot and later destroyed. The present Crusader church is one of the finest examples of Crusader-type church architecture in the purest Romanesque style. Twenty feet beneath the floor is a grotto or cave, the traditional site of the house of Joachim and Anna, the parents of the Virgin Mary (Luke 2:36). At the altar in the grotto is the image of a little child in a cradle portraying Mary and her birth in this place. For many years this site was also claimed to be the burial place of Mary.

Pool of Bethesda

In the front of the Church of St. Anne are the excavations of the Pool of Bethesda. This site was discovered in 1884 and is an authentic location. In Jesus' day it was believed that the waters had healing

Gordon's Calvary, "the place of the skull," is the traditional site of Christ's crucifixion.

A Christian pilgrim at the empty tomb, which is the traditional site of Jesus' entombment

powers when "troubled by an angel." Here Jesus healed a man who had been lame for thirty-eight years (John 5:1-19).

Excavations have revealed the five porches, one on each of the four sides and one in the middle. However no intermittent spring has been discovered as might be assumed necessary to create the "troubling of the waters." A Byzantine church and later a Crusader church once stood on this site. At the entranceway to the Pool of Bethesda, on ancient church walls, has been found a written account of this miracle in 120 languages!

As you walk from Stephen's Gate along the main street you are in the area of the *Fortress of Antonio*. This Fortress was built by Herod the Great and named to honor his friend, Mark Antony. Built on the site of an earlier defense (Neh. 2:8) it protected the northern approach to the city. Steep hills and walls protected the other three sides.

Ecce Homo Arch

Entering the chapel of the Sisters of Zion on the right, you are shown the base of an ancient arch dating back at least to the time of Hadrian (A.D. 117-138). As early as the second century A.D. this was identified as the spot in the Fortress of Antonio where Pilate spoke to the Jews saying, "Behold, the man" (John 19:5). So today it is called the "Ecce Homo" (Latin for "Behold the man") arch.

The Pavement

Inside the convent you descend a flight of steps to a level ten feet below the present streets of Jerusalem. Excavations here have uncovered the pavement of John 19:13-17. This large open courtyard of huge pavement stones is today as it was two thousand years ago. But, of course, the buildings that surrounded this courtyard in Pilate's day are gone. When Jesus was arrested, he was brought to this very area, and here he was taunted and scourged by the Roman guards. Pilate's judgment seat was probably to the side of this pavement.

On the left are steps that led to the barracks of the soldiers. In front of these steps we find the evidence of a game *Basilikos* (Latin for "king") that Roman soldiers played (the engraved figures in the stone, a circle, a crown, a sword, the Latin letter 'B'). Here the soldiers played the game similar to hopscotch, casting dice and moving across the pavement squares to arrive at a spot where the crown is carved in the stone. This game of "king" probably suggested to the Roman soldiers the torture and abuse they inflicted upon Jesus as they crowned him with thorns and placed him on a mock throne.

At the far edge of the pavement is a roadway, the actual street surface of Jesus' day. The stones have been scored to give a corrugated effect to keep the horses from slipping. There is little doubt but that here Jesus took up his cross, walked over these very stones and began his journey to Calvary! A beautiful contemporary wall mosaic showing Jesus bearing his cross commemorates this significant site. (References for this series of events are Mark 15; Matt. 27; Luke 23; John 18:18 ff.)

Every time I visit this site I am deeply moved with the awesome realization that as I kneel in prayer my knees could be pressing against the very stone touched by the feet of my Savior as he took up his cross and went out to Calvary to die in my stead! As a group of us on a recent visit here were softly singing, "Must Jesus bear the cross alone, and all the world go free," a grey-haired grandmother suddenly shouted with unrestrained joy and ecstasy, "Glory, oh glory!" And amid unrestrained emotion and free-flowing tears we did feel the presence of the living Christ in our hearts as never before and we committed ourselves anew to the way of his cross!

The apostle Paul was also imprisoned here (Acts 22:22 ff). Soldiers rescued Paul from the rioters in the Temple area, outside to the left. He was brought up the steps into this barracks area, examined, and imprisoned for safekeeping. While here Paul received a reassuring word from God and a warning of a plot to lynch him. He was quickly transferred under heavy guard from here to Caesarea (Act 23).

Via Dolorosa

You leave the convent of the Sisters of Zion to walk the Via Dolorosa (or Way of Sorrow). From the time of the Crusaders, Christian pilgrims have retraced the

t Jerusalem the city wall and the Damascus Gate

An Arab woman passing the Damascus Gate

Pool of Bethesda, where the miracu- healing (John 5) took place

Typical of Muslim architecture is this public fountain built by Sultan Quyt-bay in 1482.

path of Jesus from Pilate's prisonhouse to the cross. Usually on Fridays at 3:00 P.M., an organized procession, led by Franciscan monks, follow along this way, stopping at each of the fourteen stations of the cross.

Of course, many feet of debris have filled in and changed the streets of Jesus' day so these stations are traditional and symbolic rather than factually authentic. They are:

(1) Jesus is condemned to death.
(2) Jesus receives the cross.
(3) Jesus falls the first time.
(4) Jesus meets his mother.
(5) Simon is made to bear the cross.
(6) Veronica wipes the face of Jesus.
(7) Jesus falls the second time.
(8) Jesus meets the women of Jerusalem.
(9) Jesus falls the third time.
(10) Jesus is stripped of his garments.
(11) Jesus is nailed to the cross.
(12) Jesus dies on the cross.
(13) Jesus is taken down from the cross.
(14) Jesus is laid in the sepulchre.

Church of the Holy Sepulcher

The last five stations of the cross on this Via Dolorosa are in the Church of the Holy Sepulcher. This is a most sacred spot for the great multitudes who have come here through the centuries. They believe that underneath the roof of this church is to be found the place of the crucifixion, the burial, and the resurrection of Jesus.

The first church was built here in A.D. 335 by Constantine after Helena, the queen mother, had identified the site. There has been a church on this spot continually since that time. The present church contains some construction that dates back to the eleventh century A.D. As one church fell into disrepair, another was built or additions made. Even today you observe constant repairs and reconstruction. Various sections of the building belong to six different religious communities.

Inside the church you climb a circular stairway up a fourteen-foot hillock to the traditional spot of Calvary. The chapel immediately to the front belongs to the Roman Catholic Church. This is the Chapel of the Nailing to the Cross. The mosaic portrays a carpenter nailing Jesus to the cross while Mary Magdalene and Mary the mother of Jesus watch.

The Greek Orthodox altar is the Chapel of Calvary itself. Underneath the altar is a hole in the rock where it is believed the cross of Jesus was erected. The holes on each side are for the other two crosses.

At the foot of these steps is a large slab of marble, the Stone of the Anointing, believed to be the stone on which the body of Christ was laid out, spiced, and wrapped for burial. Here devout pilgrims often kneel, to rub a rosary over the stone, kiss the stone, and with their hands seemingly scoop up an invisible blessed substance from off the stone to spread upon their bodies. At Easter time when the crucifixion is reenacted, an actual image is nailed to the cross, then taken down in a sheet, laid on the stone, prepared for burial, and placed in the tomb.

Inside the church under the main dome is the traditional tomb itself. This site marks the end of the Via Dolorosa, the last of fourteen "stations of the cross."

In a chapel to the side is a benchlike altar and the *Pillar of Flagellation* brought here from the Fortress of Antonio. It is believed by many that Christ was tied to this pillar when he was beaten by Pilate's soldiers.

The tradition which established the Church of the Holy Sepulcher on this site is as follows: Helena, the mother of Constantine, came to the Holy Land to discover the sacred spots and memoralize them by building churches. Some say that this spot was revealed to her in a dream. Others say that a certain pious Jerusalem Jew possessed documents inherited from his father that told of this location. It is known that the Roman emperor, Hadrian, after the second revolt of the Jews, had rebuilt Jerusalem. An early tradition says that he erected a temple to Venus at Calvary so that when Christians came to worship at this site, they would appear to be bowing their knee to Venus, the goddess of love. Thus the emperor believed that soon this spot would be forgotten because Christians would refuse to bow before the statue of Venus.

Helena is reported to have led excavations at this

Rachel's Tomb at Bethlehem

The entrance to the Church of the Nativity at Bethlehem

Golgotha (Calvary) means "place of the skull," and looks like it.

The Garden of Gethsemane dotted with olive trees

spot where the temple of Venus supposedly stood. Digging through the debris, she discovered a cave containing three crosses and a plaque reading "This is Jesus, the King of the Jews." However, the plaque was not attached to any one of the crosses. Consequently, Helena could not determine which was the cross of Jesus.

According to tradition, Machaerius, the bishop of Jerusalem, suggested that the three crosses be brought in contact with the body of a certain local woman who had an incurable disease. When the first and second crosses touched her, nothing happened. But when the third cross was brought near to her body, she was miraculously healed! Thus all knew that this was the true cross on which Jesus was crucified. Nails were also found here and it is said that Constantine used some of these nails to fashion a bridle bit for his horse. He also incorporated others of the nails in a statue of himself with the belief that their presence would insure eternal permanence.

It must be left to personal judgment as to whether one accepts these traditions or accepts the setting of Gordon's Calvary and the garden tomb as the authentic site. In either case, the fact that we cannot absolutely affirm the exact location of the crucifixion, burial, and resurrection of Christ does not in any way diminish the eternal fact and reality of Jesus. The physical site is but a symbol of an even greater reality—the certainty of the living presence in our lives of a resurrected Lord!

3

From the Mount of Olives to Museums

Today's tour begins with a drive to the crest of the Mount of Olives (or Olivet) a mile-long ridge of rounded limestone hills paralleling the eastern edge of Jerusalem.

From this vantage point you have a magnificent panoramic view of the city. In the foreground, next to the multi-domed building is the *Garden of Gethsemane.* Below is the *Valley Kidron.* To the right in the eastern wall is *Stephen's Gate* where he was stoned.

Midway in the Old City wall is the *Golden Gate* (or Gate Beautiful). Beside this gate Peter and John healed the lame man while on the way to the Temple to pray (Acts 3:1-10). The Golden Gate was sealed during the Turkish occupation because of Christian expectations that Christ would return as the Prince of Peace through this gate (Ezek. 44:1-3). To the left at the southeast corner the foundations of the wall clearly show tiers of large rectangular stones, the Herodian masonry of the original wall of Jesus' day.

Directly in front is the Temple area. The golden dome is the Muslim mosque, the *Dome of the Rock.* The smaller silver dome to the left is the *Mosque of El Aksa* (the "distant mosque"). The tower, capped

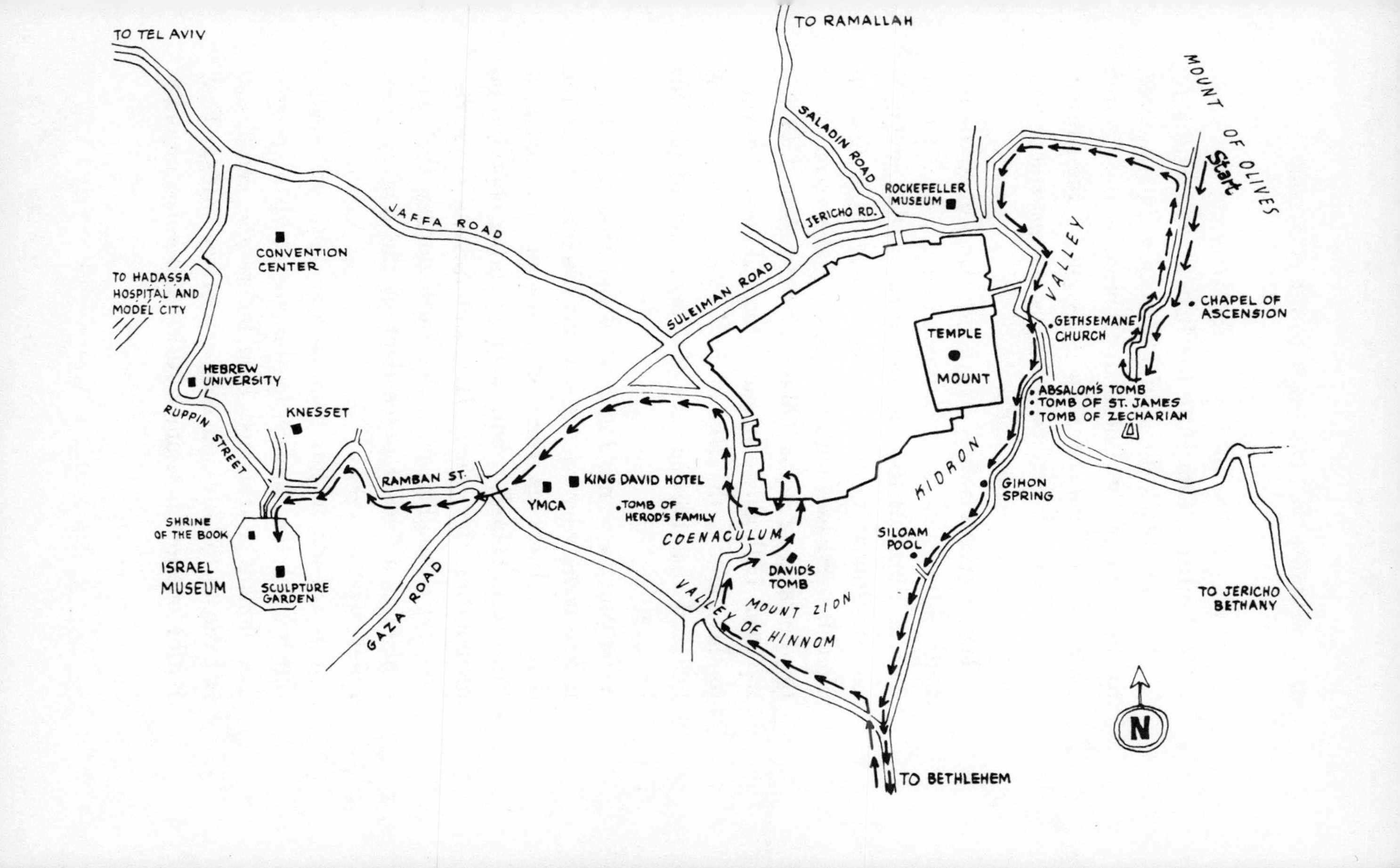
TO TEL AVIV
TO RAMALLAH
MOUNT OF OLIVES
Start
SALADIN ROAD
ROCKEFELLER MUSEUM
JERICHO RD.
JAFFA ROAD
VALLEY
CONVENTION CENTER
TO HADASSA HOSPITAL AND MODEL CITY
SULEIMAN ROAD
CHAPEL OF ASCENSION
GETHSEMANE CHURCH
TEMPLE MOUNT
HEBREW UNIVERSITY
RUPPIN STREET
KNESSET
ABSALOM'S TOMB
TOMB OF ST. JAMES
TOMB OF ZECHARIAH
KIDRON
RAMBAN ST.
KING DAVID HOTEL
YMCA
TOMB OF HEROD'S FAMILY
GIHON SPRING
SHRINE OF THE BOOK
ISRAEL MUSEUM
SCULPTURE GARDEN
COENACULUM
SILOAM POOL
DAVID'S TOMB
GAZA ROAD
VALLEY OF HINNOM
MOUNT ZION
TO JERICHO BETHANY
N
TO BETHLEHEM

by a pyramid directly beyond the Dome of the Rock, is the Lutheran *Church of the Redeemer.*

The large black dome and a smaller lighter dome, to the right of the Lutheran Church, is the *Church of the Holy Sepulcher.* To the right of the Muslim minaret beyond Stephen's Gate is the *pavement* area of Pilate's Judgment Hall.

The deep-cut valley that joins the Kidron to the south is the *Valley of Hinnom* (Jer. 7:32; 2 Chron. 28:3; 2 Kings 23:10). In the angle of the joining is the traditional spot of *Potter's Field* (the field of blood), purchased with the money Judas received for the betrayal of Jesus (Matt. 27:6 ff; Acts 1:18 ff). A Greek Orthodox convent is located there. Beyond to the south is the *Hill of Evil Council* where it is believed that the enemies of Christ met to plot his betrayal.

To your back over the crest of the Mount of Olives is *Bethpage,* where Jesus sent his disciples to get the donkey colt for his triumphal entry into Jerusalem. A Franciscan church is built over an earlier church commemorating this event. Here enterprising boys offer you, for a small price, a ride on a donkey that they explain is a "direct descendant of the donkey Jesus rode!"

You are not in this country long until you realize the role of the donkey in the life of these people. The donkey was tamed long before the camel and is basic to the life and economy of the Middle East. Eating one-fourth as much barley as a horse, a donkey is available to the poorest of families. It is not a stupid animal. The donkey needs only a halter to guide it and frequently finds its own way across stony deserts where a path can scarcely be detected. The family donkey is not only used for transportation, but helps in plowing and hauling. The Bible forbade hitching a donkey and an ox together (Deut. 22:10).

It is most appropriate that Jesus rode a donkey in his triumphal entry. For the donkey is servant of all. He is the most humble of creatures. He is the burden-bearer of the land. Jesus was to make himself a servant and a sin-bearer of all men!

Imagine the scene that took place in this area before you. Jesus is coming through the low saddle in the Mount of Olives to the right. Riding a donkey, he descends along a twisting path down the hillside, across the Kidron and up into the city through the Golden Gate. The great crowds are gathered waving palm branches, spreading their clothes before him to make a pathway and crying, "Hosanna to the Son of David" (Matt. 21:1 ff; Mark 11:1 ff; Luke 19:28 ff). On Palm Sunday each year a great procession of pilgrims follow along this way in the steps of Jesus to commemorate this event!

The Mount of Olives is mentioned only occasionally in the Old Testament. David fled over it barefooted when his son Absalom revolted (2 Sam. 15:30). Ezekiel 11:23 and Zechariah 14:4 are other references.

Jesus came often to the Mount of Olives to pray, to teach, or to pass over into the city from Bethany

An ancient cave in the Shepherd's Fields near Jerusalem, a traditional site of where angels announced Christ's birth

The Church of the Nativity at Bethlehem, built by Constantine and rebuilt by Justinian

(John 7:53; 8:1). After the Lord's Supper in the upper room, Jesus and the eleven went to the Mount of Olives (Matt. 26:30). And possibly from this same vantage point Jesus viewed this beautiful city and the magnificent Temple area and wept with unrestrained emotion over the city's rejection of his messiahship and its forthcoming destruction (Matt. 24:25).

The Chapel of the Ascension

From here you return north along the crest of the mount to the octagonal-shaped Byzantine Chapel of the Ascension on the right. This chapel is built over an exposed rock marking a high point on the Mount of Olives. There is a tradition that the foot-shaped depression in the rock is the footprint of Jesus where he last stood before ascending into heaven (Acts 1:8-13). Tradition or fact, this is certainly the Mount of Olives!

From this, or some other spot very nearby, our Lord delivered the Great Commission and ascended out of the disciples' sight into heaven! Here two men in white appeared promising, "This same Jesus shall in like manner return!" One of the spiritual highlights of a visit to this Mount is to read this passage of Scripture on this site and hear a soloist sing "The King Is Coming!"

The Garden of Gethsemane

Coming down from the Mount of Olives you stop in the Kidron Valley at the garden of Gethsemane (meaning "olive press"). This is an authentic site! From the upper room, Jesus came here with his eleven disciples to pray (John 18:1-4; Luke 22:39-53; Mark 14:32-52; Matt. 26:36-56). Today, olive groves owned by the Armenian, Greek, Russian, and Catholic churches mark this sacred site.

The roots of eight ancient olive trees in the Franciscan garden have been judged by competent authorities to be over two thousand years old. It is surely possible that one of these very olive trees sheltered our Lord as he prayed in this garden, "Not my will but thine be done."

The church by the garden is the *Basilica of the Agony* (commonly known as the Church of All Nations, for nations of the world contributed to its construction). One of the twelve domes (in the southwest corner) commemorates the contribution of the United States. The dome is decorated with the Crusader cross in the center and the American Eagle and the Seal of the United States on the sides.

This present church was constructed on the site of an older Byzantine church. (The dark stones in the floor are from the foundation of that church.) A Crusader church was also erected on this site. Near the altar is an outcrop of rock, enclosed with a low metal guardrail. This rock is believed to be the actual spot where Jesus knelt in the garden to pray. The three mosaics above the altar commemorate this event: in the center, Jesus praying; on the left, his betrayal; on the right, his arrest by the soldiers.

The Valley Kidron

From here you continue down the Valley Kidron (also called the Valley of Jehoshaphat). On the left are several mausoleums or tombs carved out of the mountainside. The cone-topped tomb is *Absalom's Pillar* (2 Sam. 18:18). There is a Jewish tradition that Absalom built this memorial to himself and is buried here. Jews passing the pillar, often threw stones and uttered curses against Absalom, the rebellious son of David. However, the Bible says that Absalom was killed while hanging by his hair from the limb of a tree in the woods of Ephraim—on the other side of the Jordan—and that he was probably buried in that area. Furthermore, we know this tomb was constructed in the Hellenistic period several centuries after Absalom's time.

The second tomb cut out of the rock with a facade of classical Doric columns is the Tomb of St. James, where many believe that James, the apostle, and first pastor of the church in Jerusalem is buried.

The pyramid-topped mausoleum is traditionally called the Tomb of Zechariah. However, an inscription on this tomb identifies it as the burial place of a priestly family called Bene Hezir.

According to both Jewish and Muslim tradition, this valley will be the scene of the last judgment. For centuries, therefore, burial in this valley has been greatly desired by devout believers of both faiths. At the time of Jesus and even more so today, tombstones and sepulchers cover the slopes on both sides of the Kidron. This fact gives vivid substance to what Jesus said to the Pharisees, "You are like whitened sepulchers, clean on the outside but inside full of defilement." As Jesus spoke these words in the Temple, how easily he could point in the direction of Kidron at these white gravestones to illustrate this dramatic figure of speech! (Matt. 23:27-29).

For centuries the Kidron and Hinnom Valleys have been a dumping place for the people of Jerusalem. Righteous Hebrew kings dumped idols and refuse from heathen shrines into Kidron (1 Kings 15:13; 2 Kings 23:4-6; 2 Chron. 29:16; 30:14). Archaeologists have determined that as much as eighty feet of debris has filled the Kidron Valley through the centuries!

Where the Kidron and Hinnom Valleys join is called Gehenna. In Jesus' day Gehenna was a garbage heap and refuse pile that was continually smoking, smoldering, and burning. It became an apt figure for the description of hell (Matt. 5:22; 10:28; 18:8 ff; 25:30; 46; Mark 9:43-48).

In the Valley Kidron on the right is the only spring around Jerusalem, called *Gihon* (or the *Virgin's Fountain*). This spring was the chief source of water for David's city and is still flowing today. The great depth of human debris in the valley is clearly evident from the fact that formerly this spring ran out the hillside and down into the valley. But today you must descend from ground level down two flights of steps into the spring.

The first occupants of the land were shepherds who

came to this spring to water their flocks. A walled Jehusite city developd here as early as 2,000 B.C. This was Salem, the city visited by Abraham, and later called Jerusalem. During the Jebusite era a tunnel was dug from the surface of this hill sloping down to a perpendicular shaft directly above the spring. The women of the city walked down the sloping tunnel, dropped their buckets down the shaft to draw water and returned inside the city walls. Some authorities believe that David entered the Jebusite city via this old Jebusite shaft and tunnel when he captured Jerusalem (2 Sam. 5:8; 1 Chron. 11:6). Directly above this spring was David's city. The foundations of the ancient walls still remain.

Here beside the spring of *Gihon,* Solomon was anointed king while the aged David remained in his palace inside the city. Nathan the prophet, Zadoc the priest, and the people witnessed the ceremony (1 Kings 1:33-45).

In 701 B.C., when Jerusalem faced a possible invasion by the Assyrian army of Sennacherib, King Hezekiah designed and accomplished a remarkable engineering feat to protect the capital's water supply. A tunnel, 1777 feet long, 6 feet high, and 2 feet wide was cut through the solid rock of this hill from Gihon to the Pool of Siloam inside the city walls. Thus water from this spring was brought underneath the hill to a protected outlet inside the city wall (2 Chron. 32:4-30; 2 Kings 20:20).

In 1880 at the other end of this tunnel an ancient

The author kneels beneath one of the ancient olive trees in the Garden of Gethsemane.

The monumental tombs in the Kidron Valley of Jerusalem, popularly called (l to r) Absalom's Pillar, the Tomb of St. James, and the Pyramid of Zachariah

Hebrew inscription was discovered that told of the completion of the tunnel. It was placed there in 701 B.C. It describes how this engineering feat was accomplished.

Hezekiah put a group of workmen at Gihon and another group at Siloam. At a given signal, both groups started toward each other, tunneling their way beneath Jerusalem. An inscription mentions the great event of the "day of the breakthrough." Workers from both ends could hear each other's voices and then "the picks struck one another" and the water flowed through the 1800-foot tunnel. The six-lined inscription, beautifully cut in classical Hebrew, is one of the oldest Hebrew inscriptions known. It is a most significant discovery for scholars, for it gives the style of writing at the time of Isaiah. The inscription has since been removed and is now preserved in the Turkish archaeology museum at Istanbul. If you are willing to wade water, you can walk through this tunnel without hazard today!

The *Pool of Siloam* is about a quarter of a mile further on the right up the fork of the road that leads to the Dung Gate at the southeast corner of the city wall. Jesus commanded the blind man to wash in the Pool of Siloam to be healed (John 9:7-11).

Eighteen people were killed when the Tower of Siloam fell. Jesus refers to this calamity in Luke 13:4. The ruins of a round stone structure nearby are believed by some to be the remains of that tower. Today, the pool is an open-air basin. Steps lead down to it and in it are broken columns from a Byzantine church. Ruins of an earlier church of the fifth century A.D. have been excavated north of the pool as well as remains of a Herodian bath.

Where the Hinnom and the Kidron Valleys join, a Greek Orthodox convent marks the site of *Potter's Field* or the Field of Blood (Acts 1:19; Matt. 27:6 ff). This field seems to have been a dumping place for potters. It was bought by the chief priest with the thirty pieces of silver cast at their feet by the remorseful Judas after his betrayal of Jesus. This "blood money" could not be put into the treasury. The site became the burial place of the poor and of strangers.

You continue south out of Jerusalem toward Bethlehem passing through the *Valley of Rephaim* (valley of the giants). This was the scene of two defeats inflicted by David upon the Philistines (2 Sam. 5:18-20).

Halfway to Bethlehem (on a high hill to the right) is the Greek Orthodox *Monastery of St. Elijah.* From Crusader times a legend has persisted that this is the site of a cave where the Prophet Elijah rested in his flight from Jezebel (1 Kings 19).

Nearing Bethlehem the road passes by the *fields of Boaz* on the left. Boaz was a wealthy landowner who married Ruth (the book of Ruth). Out of this union came the lineage of David and Jesus (Ruth; Matt. 1:5; Luke 3:32). The Jerusalem YMCA owns the property at the traditional site of the fields of Boaz. This area is also the traditional *Shepherd's*

Fields where the angels appeared to the shepherds proclaiming the birth of Christ (Luke 2).

As you approach Bethlehem on the right, there is a white-domed structure, the traditional tomb of Rachel, the daughter of Laban and Jacob's wife. The story of Jacob's long courtship and labor to win Rachel is one of the biblical classics (Gen. 29). Jacob erected a pillar over her grave (Gen. 35:19-20; 48:7). For nearly forty centuries this has been pointed out as the site where Rachel was buried. However, the actual present-day structure was not erected here until the twelfth century A.D. by the Crusaders.

Bethlehem

There are many Scripture references to this significant little village of Bethlehem (Josh. 19:5; 1 Sam. 16:13; 17:15, 20:6; 2 Chron. 11:6; Mic. 5:2; Matt. 2:1,6,8,15,16; Luke 2:4; John 7:42).

Bethlehem was the home of David and the "City of David" (Jerusalem at times was also called the "City of David"). Samuel anointed David king at Bethlehem.

Of course, Bethlehem's chief claim to fame is that Jesus was born here. The name itself means "City of Bread"—significant in that he was the "bread of life!" On the left of the city square beyond the courtyard is the Church of the Nativity, erected over a cave which Helena, mother of Constantine, believed to be the site where Christ was born.

The reference in Luke 2:7 indicates Christ was

born in a manger but makes no reference to a cave. However, this is not beyond the realm of possibility. Even to this day caves are often used as dwelling places of people as well as stables for animals. It is highly possible that this cave was the stable for the inn in which there was "no room" for Mary and Joseph.

Justin Martyr (second century A.D.) makes reference to Joseph taking quarters in a cave near Bethlehem. In the next century Origen refers to the location of the birthplace of Jesus as being a cave. Jerome (fourth century A.D.) says that even before the time of the Emperor Hadrian (A.D. 117-145) this cave was regarded as the place of the birth of Christ.

To stamp out Christian worship on this site, Hadrian directed that a pagan shrine be erected. So Jerome bemoans that "this most holy of all places was in the midst of a grove of Adonis" (the god of fertility). He continues, "In the very cave where the entering Christ uttered his first cry there is heard the weeping for the paramour of Venus." Thus a very early and reliable tradition seems to assure the authenticity of this site!

A Constantinian basilica was built here in A.D. 330. In the sixth century A.D. under Justinian, a larger church was constructed. Today's church is basically Justinian's church with minor alterations. At the time of the Persian invasion in A.D. 614 other buildings in this area were destroyed. But when the soldiers saw

Looking across the Vale of Hinnom toward Jerusalem

The Tomb of Lazarus at Bethany

A watchtower, still used today, built of field stones

Historic Mt. Zion, where David was anointed King

the mosiacs on the exterior of the church with figurines of the Wise Men dressed in what appeared to be Persian attire, they spared the church from destruction.

Again, at the time of the Arab conquest the church survived the invaders for the same reason. During the Turkish occupation, horses were stabled in the church. Later, the arched entranceway was blocked up and narrowed to keep out the animals.

Inside the church are four rows of columns forming two aisles on each side of the church. On the columns are portraits of various ancestors of Jesus. The mosaics in the floor date back to the fourth-century church. In one mosaic is the Greek word for fish, an early symbol of the Christian faith. The letters symbolize "Jesus Christ, God's Son and Savior."

The central altar at the front is Greek Orthodox and to the left is the Armenian Christian altar. The Armenians, a distinct nationality whose homeland borders Russia, are a very shrewd, skilled, and industrious people. They are often the goldsmiths, tailors, and shopsmiths of the Middle East.

A stairway on each side leads down to the grotto under the altar. Imbedded in the floor is a silver star representing the spot in the cave where Jesus was born. The inscription reads, "To the Virgin Mary is born Jesus." On one side of the grotto is an altar to memorialize the adoration of the Wise Men. The altar on the other side symbolizes the location of the manger.

On a recent visit to this site during the Christmas season, I found three German deaconesses dressed in their white habits seated on the steps softly singing Christmas carols. Settling down on a step above, I joined in singing.

As the English and German blended together to the strains of "Silent Night," the universal good news of the angel chorus broke through to my heart in a way I had never before realized. "Unto *you* is born a Saviour which is Christ the Lord."

As you visit this rock-hewn stable, there is the exciting possibility that the "ears of your heart" will also hear again the song of that angel band who first proclaimed the good news of the Savior to the shepherds in Bethlehem's fields.

There are other caves and recesses in this immediate area. In one of these caves the scholar Jerome lived for thirty years translating the Scriptures of Greek and Hebrew into Latin (called the *Vulgate*). This version was the only Bible of Western Christendom for many centuries until Wycliffe and others gave the world newer translations.

Today the little town of Bethlehem has a large Christian population. This church in Bethlehem is believed to be the oldest active church congregation in the world. Christians have gathered for worship on this spot continuously for more than fifteen hundred years.

Returning from Bethlehem to Jerusalem, you approach the Old City turning left up through the

The Pool of Siloam where Jesus commanded a blind man to wash

The Gihon Spring, outside the walls of Jerusalem

Valley of Hinnom. The hill on the left (to the south) is called the *Hill of the Offense* because here Solomon erected altars to pagan gods to please his heathen wives.

As early as Abraham's time this hillside was the scene of pagan worship and sacrifice. Here Abraham no doubt saw Canaanites tossing living infants into the red-hot arms of an image of Molech, made of iron and fashioned like a furnace. Excavations have revealed piles of ashes and vestiges of infant skeletons in cemeteries around these heathen altars. King Manasseh (seventh century B.C.) allowed the worship of Molech to corrupt Hebrew worship and Israelite children were offered to the fires of Molech. King Josiah destroyed the altars and the valley was proclaimed unclean because it was polluted with human bones (1 Kings 11:1-8; 2 Kings 21:6; 2 Kings 23:1-14; 2 Chron. 28:1-3).

The Hill of Zion

Your bus stops in a parking area on the Hill of Zion outside the gate. Zion is also a symbol of the heavenly Jerusalem, the city whose builder and maker is God (Heb. 11:10; 12:22). David captured the Jebusite city that was established on this hill and called it the "City of David" (1 Chron. 11:1-9). The ark of the covenant was finally brought to Jerusalem by David and remained in Zion until Solomon placed it in the Temple (1 Sam. 5:1-7:2; 2 Sam. 6:12-17; 1 Kings 8:1-11).

The Upper Room

From here you walk to the traditional upper room, scene of the Last Supper of Jesus and his disciples. The room was also the place where the apostles gathered after the ascension (Luke 22; Mark 14:14 ff; Acts 1:12-24). Many Bible scholars believe the upper room was in the home of John Mark's mother.

The present upper room (the *cenaculum*) is a large Crusader hall. No archaeological evidence authenticates this site. But an early fourth-century tradition locates the upper room near the Zion Gate. And as early as the fourth-century, a church called "The Church of the Apostles" was meeting on this site. To the Christian pilgrim today this site symbolizes that Last Supper which has great significance in our Christian faith. A visit to this site is an impressive spiritual experience.

The Tomb of David

Near the upper room is the traditional tomb of David (1 Kings 2:1-11). Authorities generally agree however that this is not where David was buried, but, it does offer a symbol to both Muslim and Jew to venerate and pay homage to King David.

Inside the Zion Gate—directly north on the left on the Street of Omar Ibn El-Khattab—is the traditional site of the *Palace of Caiaphas* (John 18:24). Caiaphas was the son-in-law of the high priest Annas. After his arrest, Jesus was brought from the residence of the high priest Annas to the palace of Caiaphas and then taken to the judgment hall of Pilate.

Caiaphas, jealous of the popularity of Jesus after the raising of Lazarus, made a statement to the priests and Pharisees which ultimately led to the crucifixion of Jesus. "It is expedient for us that one man should die for the people" (John 11:50). When Peter gained popularity with the people by healing the lame man at the Temple gate, Caiaphas and his colleagues dared not punish the apostles (Acts 4:7-21).

The identification of this site as the house of Caiaphas dates from A.D. 333, although there is no archaeological evidence to validate this tradition. This obviously was the residence of a very prominent person of the Roman era. It probably gives us a good idea of what the residence of Caiaphas was like.

Further north where this same street joins the entrance to the Joppa Gate on the left is the *Citadel* (*Herod's palace*). The royal palace was guarded by three massive towers that Herod named Hippicus (after his brother), Phasael (a friend), and Mariamne (his wife). When Titus destroyed the city in A.D. 70 he left these three towers standing. The Crusaders erroneously identified them as the "tower of David." Today only the foundation of Phasael from Herod's day is still standing.

It was here that Herod entertained the three Wise Men and requested that they return from Bethlehem to report their visit to the infant Christ (Matt. 2:16 ff).

Some authorities believe it was here in Herod's palace (rather than the pavement area of the Fortress

ance to the Grotto of the Nativity with Crusader pilasters

The Chapel of the Ascension on the Mount of Olives

The rolling fields near Jerusalem where shepherds were "keeping watch over their flock by night" (Luke 2)

of Antonio) that Christ was brought before Pilate. In the huge open air courtyard of these impressive ruins, a dramatic "Light and Sound" performance is conducted in the summertime recounting the history of Israel.

From the Hill of Zion you drive northeast through new Jerusalem. Time permitting, a stop at *Herod's tomb* near the King David Hotel offers an excellent example of the "rolling stone" closure to a tomb. The huge circular wheel-like stone rides in a slot to easily roll downhill and lock in place. Then it is almost impossible to remove it or roll it back. The Jewish historian Josephus says that Herod the Great built a family tomb a short distance from the Jaffa Gate. While this seems to be a logical location for the tomb, it is more likely the tomb of his wife Mariamne rather than Herod.

Shrine of the Book

Continuing west past Israel's National Parliament Building, the *Knesset,* your last stop is the Israeli Museum. Here is an art museum, the Billy Rose Sculpture Garden, a biblical and archaeological museum and the Shrine of the Book.

The Shrine of the Book houses a number of the Dead Sea Scrolls and other artifacts discovered at *Qumran* (where you will visit tomorrow). Its unique architectural design captures the theme of the Scrolls, the conflict between the sons of life and the sons of darkness. The white dome symbolizes the sons of light, the black walls, the sons of darkness!

The importance of the Dead Sea Scrolls is two-fold. First, they give us new knowledge of the text of the Old Testament. Before the discovery of the Scrolls, our oldest complete manuscripts of the Hebrew Old Testament were dated tenth century A.D. The Dead Sea Scrolls have provided biblical texts in Hebrew a thousand years older than anything we have previously known (except for one small fragment).

Second, the nonbiblical scrolls throw much light on the Essenes, a people who undoubtedly had a profound effect upon the early Christian movement and the only sect of Judaism that was not condemned in the New Testament. We find the Essenes living in the wilderness to prepare the way of the Lord (Isa. 40:3). They were organized like a "Salvation Army," accepting a rigorous discipline, studying the law continually while awaiting the coming of the Promised One.

Early Christian groups in Jerusalem were influenced by the Essenes' pattern of life. They held property in common and poverty was idealized. Both observed sacramental meals. Both followed after "The Way" as they described their belief. Both criticized the Sadducees and Pharisees and considered themselves members of the new covenant. Both believed that the present life is the battleground betwen two opposing realms, good and evil, light and darkness, truth and error.

On the other hand, the Christians were radically

different. Some scholars believe the Gospel of John to be the Christian answer to the Essenes. The "good news" of God's love is quite different from the "new righteousness" of the Essenes as revealed in the Dead Sea Scrolls.

Christ was not the "teacher of righteousness"—but "a lamb, slain" to bring them into a new life. Christ suffered and died and did not reign in earthly splendor as expected by the Essene community. His saving work was for the multitudes of outcasts and sinners and not for the select few, as conceived by the Essene community. These differences are at the very heart of our Christian faith, the unique essence of that truth "God was in Christ *reconciling the world* unto himself!"

There are other museums in Jerusalem that you may visit at your leisure:

The Rockefeller Museum (Jericho Road)—established in 1938, containing a vast collection of significant antiquities.

The Clarke Collection of Antiquities (YMCA)—containing numerous prehistoric, Israelite, and Roman artifacts.

The Model City of Jerusalem (Holy Land Hotel)—a huge outdoor scaled model of Jerusalem of the second temple era.

The new *Hadassah Medical Center* where the world-famous stained glass windows portraying the twelve tribes by Russian-born Jewish artist *Marc Chagall* may be seen.

4

Bethany down to the Dead Sea

Today you will visit a geological wonder of the world, the lowest spot on the earth's surface, 1292 feet below sea level! On the floor of this great rift you will find the ancient biblical city of Jericho, Qumran where the Dead Sea Scrolls were discovered, and the Dead Sea.

Bethany

You drive east from Jerusalem through the Kidron Valley past Gethsemane and the Jewish cemeteries. Three miles out of the city is the village of Bethany. (References: Matt. 17; 21:1-2; 26:6; Mark 11; 12; 14:3; Luke 10:29; 38-42; John 11:1-44).

Bethany was the home of Mary, Martha, and Lazarus, where Jesus stayed during the last week of his ministry in Jerusalem. He walked from here over the Mount of Olives into Jerusalem in the mornings, and returned at nighttime to the home of his friends.

It was here that Jesus raised Lazarus from the dead (John 11:3). A spire topped with a cross marks the traditional spot where Martha came out to meet Jesus upon his return from the other side of Jordan at the death of Lazarus. Here in Bethany was the house of Simon the Leper where a grateful woman anointed the feet of Jesus (Mark 14:3).

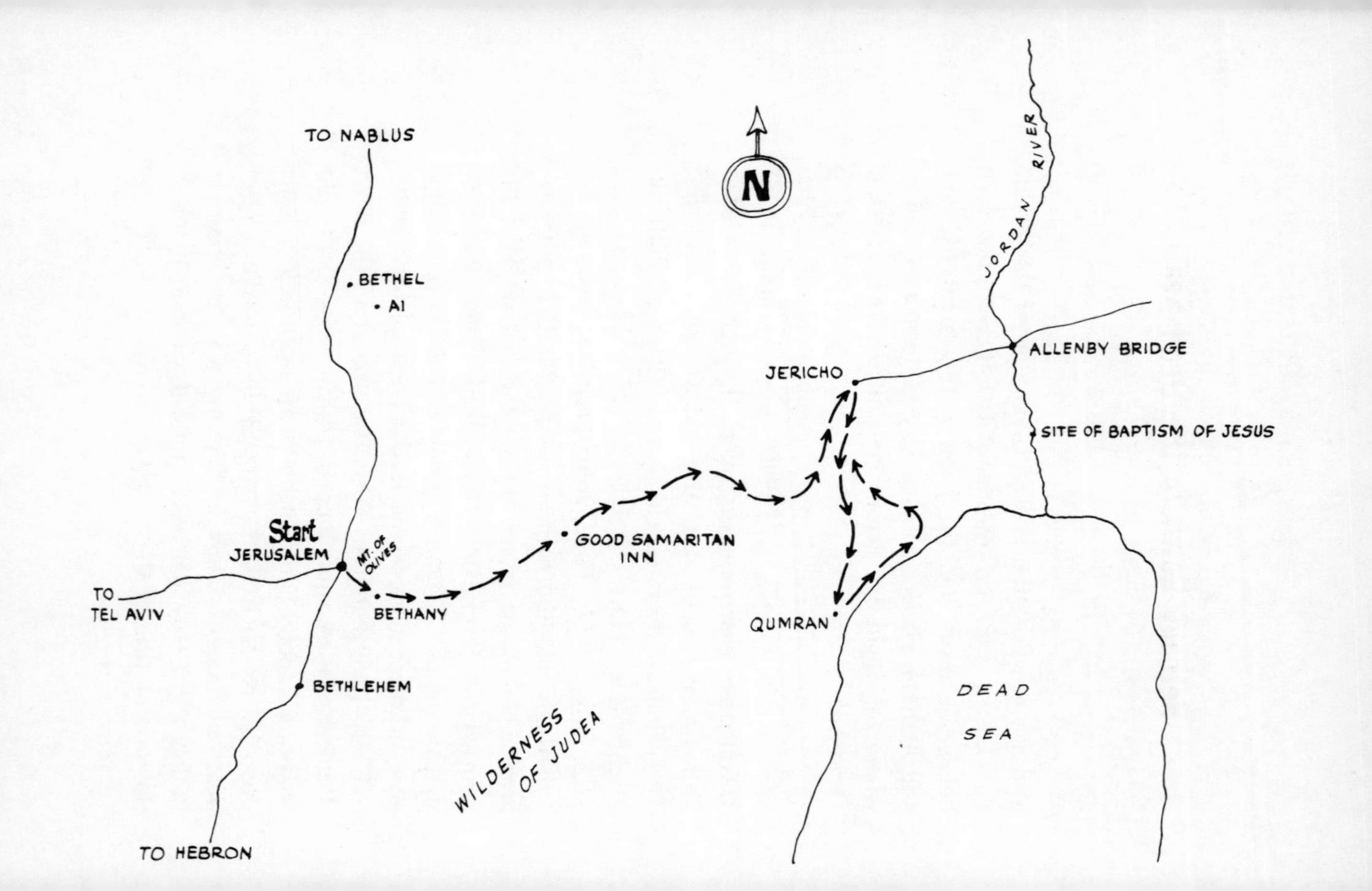
TO NABLUS
N
JORDAN RIVER
BETHEL
AI
ALLENBY BRIDGE
JERICHO
SITE OF BAPTISM OF JESUS
Start
JERUSALEM
MT. OF OLIVES
GOOD SAMARITAN INN
TO TEL AVIV
BETHANY
QUMRAN
BETHLEHEM
DEAD SEA
WILDERNESS OF JUDEA
TO HEBRON

A new church has been built on the site of excavations at the traditional location of the home of Mary and Martha. Remains of a Byzantine church and a later church have been uncovered indicating that as early as the fourth and fifth centuries A.D. this site was regarded as the home of Mary and Martha.

While it is true that Jewish tombs and houses of the first century A.D. have been excavated here, there is no factual evidence to identify any particular house as belonging to Mary and Martha. However, this is certainly the tiny village of Bethany where the friends of Jesus lived. Somewhere in this immediate area Jesus visited many times and from here he undoubtedly traveled the pathway that clearly leads from Bethany over the Mount of Olives into Jerusalem.

Tomb of Lazarus

To the right of the church a path leads up the hill to the traditional tomb of Lazarus. Because the debris of human occupation has covered the site, you must descend twenty-two steps down a narrow tunnel to arrive at the tomb. While there is no evidence that this is the actual tomb of Lazarus, it is a first-century A.D. tomb, typical and symbolic of the place where Lazarus was buried from which Jesus called him forth alive (John 11:43). It was here Jesus promised, "I am the resurrection and the life . . . and whosoever liveth and believeth in me shall never die" (John 11:25-26).

From Bethany the road continues northeast *down* to Jericho. In the short distance of 25 miles the road drops almost 3500 feet from the hills of Jerusalem with an altitude of 2500 feet to Jericho, *820 feet below sea level!*

The road twists through a vast desolate mountain wilderness. Somewhere in this area John the Baptist lived and preached (Matt. 3:1-4), and Jesus retreated during the great temptation (Matt. 4:1-11). The Jericho road has always been a dangerous road to travel. Throughout history robbers and bandits hiding in the hills have preyed upon travelers. Jerome in the fifth century A.D. called it the "way of blood." Even in the early part of this century, pilgrims traveling the Jericho road were still harassed by highwaymen. Of course, it is perfectly safe to travel today, but this fact gave the setting for Jesus' story of the good Samaritan who befriended the man beaten by robbers on the Jericho road (Luke 10:30-37).

The Inn of the Good Samaritan

Halfway between Jerusalem and Jericho on the right are the ruins of the Inn of the Good Samaritan that date back to the Crusader era. While we have no archaeological evidence to tie this site with the parable of the good Samaritan, this obviously was the site of an overnight resting place for caravans and travelers on a road that has been here since Roman times.

A few miles further down the Jericho road is the sign marking *sea level.* From this point on you are in a vast valley below the level of earth's seas! A short distance from the sign the road opens out onto a wide plain offering a splendid view of the Jordan Valley. To the right in the distance is the Dead Sea. Straight ahead is the Jericho oasis. To the left extending far to the north is the green belt of the Jordan River Valley.

Jericho

Jericho is 830 feet below sea level, with a subtropical climate and an abundant water supply from a free-flowing spring. Here, from the beginnings of time man has found an ideal living situation. In this oasis close at hand were all the basic needs of early man—water, fruits and grains, a warm and healthy climate. In Jesus' day Jericho was the winter resort for the people of Jerusalem. Here they could come and lounge in the luxury of 80° temperature in the dead of winter. Today, Jericho produces choice oranges, citrus, and other tropical fruits.

Jericho comes into biblical prominence as the first city captured by Joshua and the children of Israel in their conquest of the promised land.

To simulate the perspective of Moses, Joshua, and the children of Israel as they viewed the promised land, you must stand on *Mount Nebo,* far on the horizon to the east and slightly to the south beyond the Jordan River. From that high vantage point Joshua plotted his stategy of conquest.

The perpendicular mountainsides that you just came through formed a natural barrier protecting the Judean highlands. But these hills were broken by three valleys leading up into the central plateau. Joshua chose to march up the northern valley that went by way of Jericho, Ai, and up to Bethel. This approach appeared to be the easiest route into the highlands through which to move an army and a large number of people.

The mouth of each valley was protected by a fortress city, in this case, Jericho. Thus Jericho, the key to the interior, became Joshua's first military objective. The children of Israel marched around the walls of this stategic city once a day for six days, and on the seventh day, seven times, Then, amid the blowing of trumpets and a shout, the walls of Jericho fell down (Josh. 6).

There are three sites for three cities of Jericho. The modern village of Jericho dates from Byzantine times. About one mile from present-day Jericho are the ruins of the Jericho of Jesus' day. Your visit continues to another nearby site, the ruins of Old Testament Jericho of Joshua's day and earlier.

Extensive excavations on this *tel,* going down through seventy feet of human debris, have revealed continuous human habitation on this site back to 7000 B.C. Thus, Jericho is one of, if not the oldest, continuously inhabited village settlements to be found anywhere in the world.

The stone wall, with the round tower at the top enclosing a circular stairway, belongs to the Neolithic period. This is the oldest city wall yet discovered

Hezekiah's Tunnel at the Pool of Siloam

A "beast of burden" seeks a "breather."

The barren land of Qumran, where the Dead Sea Scrolls were found

"Cave Four" at Qumran near the Dead Sea

anywhere in the world! Standing here on the edge of this excavated trench at Jericho, you are probably viewing the first walled village that early man ever constructed in his progressive climb to civilized urban living. The bricks in the wall opposite the tower belong to the early Bronze Age or the Hyksos period. On the fringe of the mound are Iron Age walls, from the age of the kingdom of Israel and Judah.

The highest point of the mound belongs to the early Bronze Age (3000-2000 B.C.). This means that on the summit of this mound there is *nothing as late as Joshua's time!* There is no wall now showing on the tel that can be identified as the wall which fell to Joshua. Some critics would therefore discount the biblical account of the fall of Jericho. However, students of archaeology have offered several explanations. One is that the Canaanites of Joshua's day had used the earlier walls of the Middle Bronze Era to fortify their city, simply buttressing and reinforcing them.

Another explanation is that either the process of erosion or the enthusiasm of brickmakers—who took charge of the mound in succeeding centuries to manufacture mud bricks—have carried away from the top of the mound the remains of the culture of Joshua's day. The latter explanation fits in with the discovery of debris from Joshua's era on the outer fringes of this circular mound. In other words, at one time there may have been many more feet of occupational debris (which contained the ruins of Jericho of Joshua's day) piled on top of this seventy-foot mound which has

The excavations of Qumran, on the shores of the Dead Sea, occupied by the Essenes of Jesus' day

Caves at Qumran—In one of these a Bedouin shepherd found the Dead Sea Scrolls in 1947.

through the centuries been removed by the hand of man and nature.

A clue to the antiquity of this site is revealed by the realization that this huge mound of seventy feet of occupational debris was not here when the first village was built. Half of that seventy feet belongs to the pre-pottery-neolithic age which means it was put here by men before 5000 B.C.!

Excavations have revealed Neolithic Jericho man was very religious, had built a temple here, and worshiped a trio of gods (male, female, and child). The first Jericho man also had a concept of survival after death as indicated by the practice of covering the skulls of the dead with plaster to create a lifelike effect.

Elisha's Fountain

At the foot of the mound is an abundant full-flowing spring called "Elisha's Fountain" believed to be where Elisha made the bitter water sweet (2 Kings 2:19-22). This spring is responsible for the oasis in the valley. Irrigation channels carry the water throughout the area. Jericho was also the location of Elijah's school of the prophets. And from here he was taken by a whirlwind into heaven (2 Kings 2:1-11).

In the distance beyond Jericho rises a stark mountain range, the traditional site of the *mount of temptation* where Jesus was tempted (Matt. 4:1-11; Mark 1:12 ff; Luke 4:1-13). Monastic dwellings of the Byzantine era have been constructed in the caves on the face of the cliffs.

About a mile away in the direction of the mountains are the ruins of *New Testament Jericho.* This was the winter capital of Herod the Great and his son Archaleus. Excavations have revealed grand imposing buildings, Roman baths with mosaic floors, wine cellars painted in gold encrusted plaster, and a magnificent palace of Herod the Great.

It was at this Jericho where Jesus restored sight to blind Bartemaeus (Mark 14:42-52). Here the tax collector Zacchaeus climbed a sycamore tree to see Jesus. Jesus went home with him and gave the parable of the pounds (or talents) (Luke 19:1-27).

Qumran

Eight miles southeast of Jericho on the northwest shore of the Dead Sea is Qumran. In 1947 the most important archaeological discovery of the modern era was made when the Dead Sea Scrolls were found in the caves of the wild mountain range directly above Qumran.

The discovery of these scrolls led to the excavation of these ruins. Here were uncovered elaborate installations for communal life for a large group of people erected sometime during the first century B.C. A central court is surrounded by rectangular rooms including a counsel chamber with benches along its walls, a scriptorium where the scribes sat who copied the texts of the Bible and other writings, and a kitchen. To the south is a dining hall, a potter's workshop and a storehouse. Water was brought by aqueducts from

Jebel Qarantal, the traditional Mount of Temptation, as viewed from Jericho

The traditional site of Lazarus' tomb, where an Arab woman stands watch at the entrance

the nearby mountains to supply no less than eight pools. Apparently an earthquake interrupted the life of the community and leveled the buildings in 31 B.C. Later, on top of those ruins, a second series of buildings were constructed.

Qumran was occupied by a Jewish sect of Jesus' day called the Essenes (a third religious order along with the Sadducees and Pharisees). The Roman historian Pliny tells of a city of the Essenes "in the wilderness." Josephus and Philo numbered them at four thousand. Qumran is probably the location of one of the main communities of these desert dwelling Essenes. Qumran is apparently the sect's final place of exile, established by a founder called "a teacher of righteousness."

The Essenes represented a movement in Judaism that began about 145 B.C. They were disgusted and outraged by the secularization of Judaism, and returned to the wilderness to live in the desert simplicity of the Mosaic era.

In this communal and generally celibate life, they had an intense absorption in the law, the qualities of the righteous life, and a fervent expectation of the immediate fulfillment of prophecy in the coming of the Messiah and the end of the age. If John the Baptist was not a part of the Essene community of Jesus' day, he certainly was strongly influenced by them. His condemnation of the "Temple Jews," his preaching righteousness, his simple dress and diet, his desert existence—all reflect the life-style and attitude of the

Essenes who lived here at Qumran.

When Vespasian was sent by Rome to put down the Jewish rebellion, he destroyed Jericho to the north of Qumran. Then as the Roman armies marched on Qumran, the Essenes had last minute prayers, hid their sacred writings in the nearby caves, and fled to the hills never to return. Their monastic dwelling place was destroyed by Vespasian, covered by the sands of the centuries and forgotten. Their treasured writings hidden in the caves remained a secret for 1,879 years!

In the spring of 1947, a Bedouin shepherd boy was looking for a lost goat in this desolate wilderness. He threw a stone into a cave high on the mountainside. The carelessly thrown stone shattered a jar inside the cave.

Intrigued by the strange noise, the boy climbed up into the cave to investigate. Here he found pottery jars containing ancient manuscripts. Scholars eventually received the "find" and discovered among them two manuscripts of the book of Isaiah, one almost perfectly preserved. Other manuscripts were commentaries on Genesis, Habakkuk, thanksgiving psalms, and various writings related to the Essenes.

This discovery startled the biblical world. In the ensuing years hundreds of caves in this area were searched and additional manuscripts discovered. Ten different manuscript-bearing caves have been discovered in the immediate Qumran area, all producing significant archaeological "finds." Portions of over one hundred scrolls of Old Testament books have appeared.

Cave Four had fragments of every book except Esther. Scholars have dated earlier fragments to about 200 B.C. The main Isaiah scroll is dated about 100 B.C.

The ruins at Qumran and the discovery of the Dead Sea Scrolls are an eloquent demonstration of the eternal truth that all flesh is as grass, the glory of man fades away, the grass withers and then dies, but the "word of God" abides forever! (1 Pet. 1:24-25).

Across from Qumran on the opposite shore of the Dead Sea, and thirty miles to the south, lay the five cities of the plains (Gen. 13–14) which included *Sodom* and *Gomorrah.* These cities were destroyed about 1900 B.C. and an earthquake dropped the whole area into the Dead Sea.

About 2000 B.C. Abraham and Lot came into this country. Lot, seeing the productivity and fertility of the valley pitched his tent toward Sodom (Gen. 13:10). The wickedness of the Sodomites was so debasing as to become proverbial (Isa. 3:9; Lam. 4:6; Matt. 10:25; 2 Pet. 2:6; Jude 7). The account of God's destruction of the cities of Sodom and Gomorrah and the escape of Lot is recorded in Genesis 19.

The Dead Sea

In the Old Testament the Dead Sea is called the Salt Sea, the Sea of the Plain, East Sea, and Former Sea (Gen. 14:3; Num. 34:3; 13; Josh. 3:16; 12:3; 15:2; 18:10; Ezek. 47:18; Joel 2:20; Zach. 14:8). The Dead Sea is not mentioned in the New Testament, but Josephus refers to it as the Sea of Sodom. The Arabs call it the Sea of Lot.

The Dead Sea is a part of the great Rift Valley, a fracture in the earth's surface that begins here in the Middle East and extends 5000 miles down through the African continent. The Dead Sea is 46 miles long and 9½ miles wide, lying 1292 feet below sea level (the lowest place on the earth's surface) and has a depth of 1312 feet. It is fed by the Jordan.

The Dead Sea has no outlet for its waters except by evaporation. This has through the centuries resulted in a concentration of minerals (magnesium, calcium, sodium, potash, etc.) in suspension five times greater than ocean water. It is called the Dead Sea because no organic life survives in the water.

Four miles north of Qumran on the shores of the Dead Sea is a beach resort area, a pleasant last stop on today's journey. Here is an airconditioned restaurant and a bath house with showers and rental bathing suits. You may climax your day with a swim in these strange waters of the Dead Sea where it is impossible to sink!

5

Armageddon to Caesarea

Today you visit Haifa, Israel's harbor city on the slopes of Mt. Carmel. Enroute you will visit the fabulous ruins of Megiddo and Caesarea by the Sea.

Leaving Jerusalem by the main highway to Tel Aviv you pass through vast groves of pine, cypress, and eucalyptus trees that have been planted in recent years as a part of Israel's land reclamation program.

About twelve miles from Jerusalem, the road descends into the *Valley of Ajalon* (where Joshua commanded the sun to stand still, Josh. 10:12-23). The country to the south is the land of Samson. His home was at *Zorah* about three miles off this main road.

At *Ramla* the road forks to the north (the left fork continues into Tel Aviv). Ramla is the traditional site of the home of Joseph of Arimathea.

Passing *Lod,* Israel's international airport, you enter the *Sharon Valley.* Just beyond *Petah Tigva* on the right are the ruins of the fortress of *Antipatris,* built by Herod and named after his father. Paul was brought here on his way to Caesarea for trial before the Roman governor (Acts 23). Here also the Philistines captured the ark of the covenant (1 Sam. 4:1-11). In these *Plains of Sharon* David tended his sheep (1 Chron. 27:29).

At *Hadera,* the main road continues north to Haifa

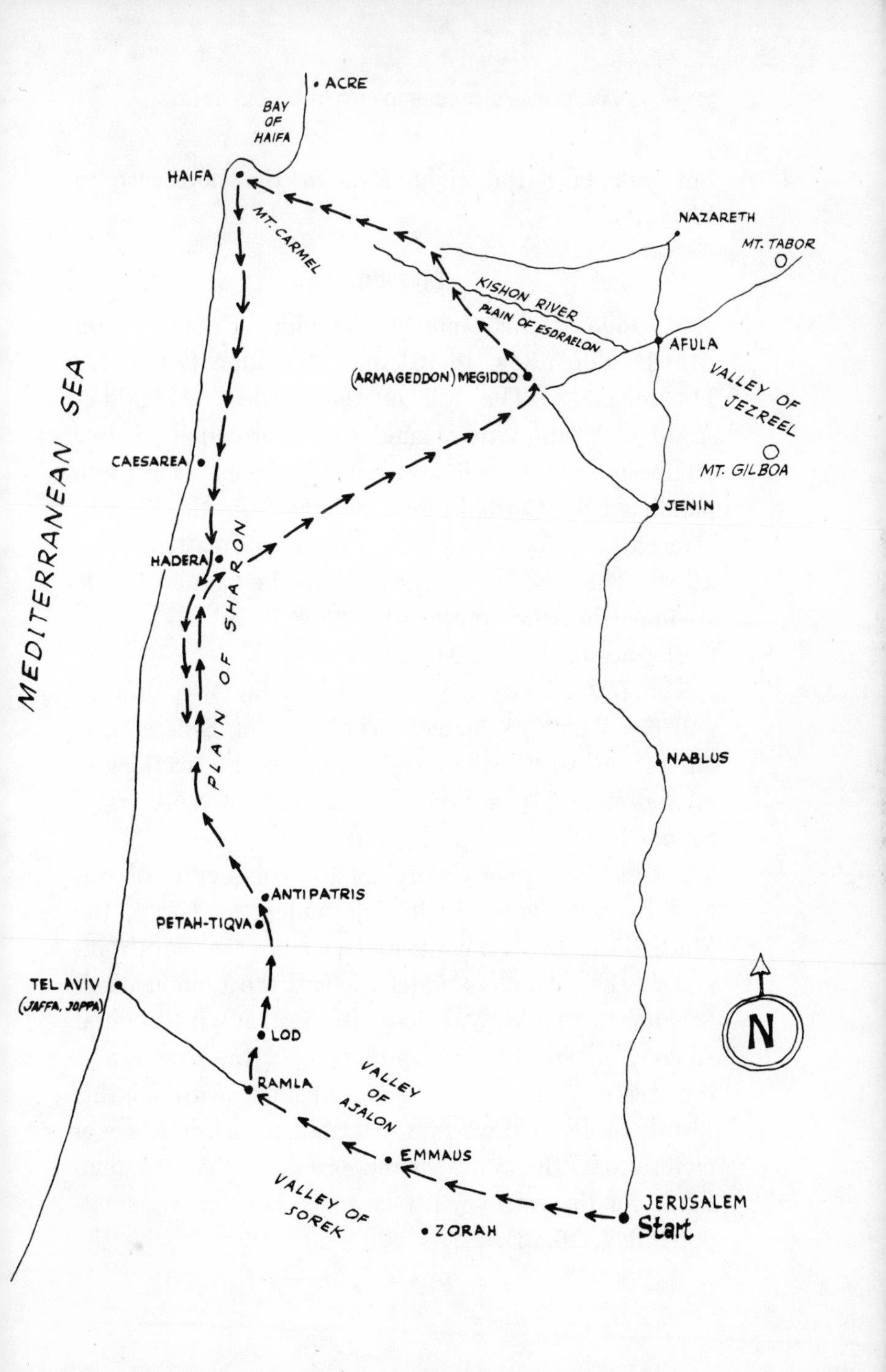
ACRE
BAY OF HAIFA
HAIFA
MT. CARMEL
NAZARETH
MT. TABOR
KISHON RIVER
PLAIN OF ESDRAELON
AFULA
VALLEY OF JEZREEL
(ARMAGEDDON) MEGIDDO
MEDITERRANEAN SEA
CAESAREA
MT. GILBOA
JENIN
HADERA
PLAIN OF SHARON
NABLUS
ANTIPATRIS
PETAH-TIQVA
TEL AVIV
(JAFFA, JOPPA)
N
LOD
RAMLA
VALLEY OF AJALON
EMMAUS
VALLEY OF SOREK
ZORAH
JERUSALEM
Start

but you take the right fork to the northeast to Megiddo.

Megiddo

Megiddo is the same as the older Hebrew word Armageddon (Rev. 16:16) and Megiddon (Zach. 12: 11) meaning "The hill of the battles." Megiddo's strategic location dominated the intersection of two vitally important trade and military routes. One route paralleled the Carmel range running from the Phoenician cities of Tyre and Sidon, south and east to Jerusalem. The other route cut through the Carmel Range coming from the southwest out of Egypt and going to the northeast into Mesopotamia.

This fortress city overlooks the Plains of Esdraelon and the Valley of Jezreel. The Plain of Esdraelon is one of the most fertile farming and grazing sections in all Palestine. It is blessed with an abundant water supply from natural wells and springs.

Across these plains marched the conquerors of history: Xerxes, Sennacherib, Alexander the Great, the Maccabees, the Romans under Titus, the Arab invaders, the Crusaders under Richard the Lion-hearted, Saladin, the Turks, Napoleon, the British with General Allenby in World War I, and last of all, the Israelis and the Arabs. Thus it is significant that, with all this history of decisive warfare determining the destinies of civilizations, the Bible should prophesy that the final battle for the world will take place here at Armageddon (Rev. 16:16).

The first fortress city on this site was built on bedrock in about 3500 B.C.; the last, the twentieth city, was built on the seventy-foot high rubble of its predecessors and was destroyed in 450 B.C. Major excavations have been conducted here to uncover the remains of Solomon's chariot city; ruins of the palaces of the Assyrians who ruled Galilee from this location; a pagan temple to Astarte (1050 B.C.); three earlier Canaanite temples; and evidence of Neolithic or late Stone Age people in artifacts of chipped flints and tools (about 8000-4500 B.C.).

There are many biblical references to Megiddo. Joshua slew the king of Megiddo in the conquest of the land (Josh. 12:21) and gave Megiddo and her towns to Manasseh (Josh. 17:11). However, the inhabitants of the city were not dislodged until later when the children of Israel were waxen strong (Judg. 1:27). The forces of Deborah and Barak defeated the Cananite King Jabin and Israel temporarily gained Megiddo (about 1150 B.C., Judg. 4).

Solomon made the city the headquarters for his horsemen and chariots (1 Kings 9:15; 10:26-29; 2 Chron. 1:14-17; 9:25). Egypt occupied the city in 915 B.C. (1 Kings 14:25; 2 Chron. 12:9). In this conquest, they took away the treasures of the Temple and the palace in the fifth year of Rehoboam. King Ahaziah died at Megiddo about 842 B.C. (2 Kings 9:27). At Megiddo King Josiah met his untimely death against the Egyptians (2 Kings 23:29; 2 Chron. 35:22).

Ahab enlarged the stables of Solomon to accommo-

Looking north from the tel of Megiddo across the Plains of Armageddon.

"Cup" of the 23rd Psalm—David may have had this kind of "cup" in mind

Stone manger from Solomon's stables Megiddo

date 450 horses and 150 chariots. Excavations of Solomon's Megiddo have revealed stone-paved ramps used by Solomon's chariots, a magnificent fortified gate, massive walls and ramparts, a palace and chariot stables with horse watering-troughs. A huge circular grain silo with an interior stairway built by Ahab has been uncovered. But perhaps the most impressive site at Megiddo is an ingenuous water system developed by ancient engineers in about 1198 B.C. It is uncertain whether the builders were Hittite, Egyptian, or Canaanite.

Inside the city a vertical shaft with a winding staircase is cut downward 120 feet to join a horizontal tunnel which runs out to a camouflaged water supply. By these stairs and this tunnel the inhabitants of Megiddo were able to obtain water in a time of siege. The walk down the steps of this shaft from atop the mound and out through the tunnel to arrive at ground level outside the city is a never-to-be-forgotten experience!

From Megiddo we follow the road to Haifa twenty miles to the northwest, skirting the foothills of the *Mt. Carmel Range* that rises to the east on the left. The road passes through the fertile valley of Esdraelon (or Jezreel Valley) which stretches all the way to Nazareth in the north, the Jordan Valley to the east, and the coastal areas above the Carmel range on the west.

This was a very wealthy section in Jesus' day, the center of *Galilee,* inhabited by three million people.

The people of this area accepted Judaism only one hundred years before the time of Jesus. Although it was a comparatively new religion, the Galileans took to Judaism readily and almost every village had a synagogue. The synagogue was a Babylonian institution adopted by the Jews during the captivity and brought back as an enduring institution of Judaism. From the synagogue came the Christian concept of a church and the Moslem concept of a mosque.

About halfway to Haifa the road runs parallel with the *Kishon River* entering into the Valley of Zebulon (the territory given to the tribe of Zebulon, Judg. 1:27-30; 4:10-16). In this plain near the Kishon River Elijah slew the four hundred prophets of Baal (1 Kings 18). It was down through this valley that Elijah ran in front of the chariot of Ahab in his flight from Jezebel after his contest with the prophets of Baal on Mt. Carmel.

From here Mt. Carmel is clearly seen in the distance to the east. A monastery sits on top of the mountain at the traditional site of Elijah's contest with the 450 priests of Baal and 400 prophets of Asherah. Here Elijah called down fire from heaven to destroy the water-drenched altars and demonstrate the power of Jehovah.

Asherah was a female goddess of Tyre. Baal was the chief member of the Canaanite family of gods and was the farm god, responsible for the germination of the crops, the increase of flocks, and the fertility of farm families.

A Roman aqueduct leading from Mt. Hermon to Caesarea

Roman amphitheater at Caesarea by the sea

Herodian stones and Roman columns built into a Crusader fort at Caesarea

Another haunting view of the seashore at Caesarea

Worshipers of Baal indulged in licentious dances, ritualistic meals, and orgies of sexual license performed around the rustic altars and in sacred groves. Hebrew prophets for three centuries protested against the apostasy of the children of Israel as elements of Baal-ism and immorality crept into their practice of religion. Jezebel, daughter of the king of Tyre (present-day Lebanon to the north) and wife of King Ahab, was one of the most fanatical worshipers of Baal. Elijah's victory in the contest with her prophets on Mt. Carmel represented the great vindication and supremacy of Jehovah!

Haifa

The Carmel range extends from the hills of Samaria to the Mediterranean. The highest peak is 1810 feet.

The headland of the mountain range at the sea coast rises 556 feet above the modern coastal city of Haifa. Haifa is a thriving modern shipping and commercial center.

Circling to the north is a crescent-shaped bay with the sister city of *Acre* on the opposite tip. Paul stayed one day in Acre (Acts 21:7). Eighty thousand Cru-saders died in the battle to capture Acre and gain control of this strategic natural harbor.

The Bahai Temple

In Haifa is located a magnificent gold-domed temple set in a luxurious Persian garden, the world center of the Bahai religion. This religion was established in

1844 in Persia (present-day Iran) by a prophet calling himself "The Bab." The religion draws heavily from Muslim tradition but claims to be a synthesis of the best of all religion. In the past century the religion has become worldwide with local centers in most every country.

Haifa has several museums of interest to the biblical student:

The Ethnological and Folklore Museum (Arlosoroff St.) with exhibits portraying the culture and religion of the Jews and Palestinian Arabs.

The Maritime Museum (Ha-Namal St.) containing models of ancient ships and other maritime artifacts.

The Museum of Ancient Art (Town Hall) with exhibits of sculpture, pottery, figurines, coins, textiles.

The Prehistoric and Natural History Museum (Hatishby St.) with artifacts and dioramas of Neolithic man. In the caves of the Carmel ridge have been found prehistoric human remains, artifacts, and skulls that archaeologists have identified as Carmelite man, an ancient creature.

Caesarea

From Haifa you take the coastal road thirty miles due south to Caesarea.

Caesarea by the sea (not to be confused with Caesarea Philippi) was a very important Roman city. It was built between 25 and 13 B.C. by Herod the Great on a site called Strato's Tower, an ancient Phoenician stronghold. Named after Caesar Augustus, Caesarea was a beautiful city eclipsing Jerusalem in magnificence and in political importance. It was the seat of the Roman procurators. Here in A.D. 69 the Roman general Vespasian was crowned emperor in the midst of his conquest of Palestine to suppress the Jewish rebellion. He returned to Rome and his son Titus completed the campaign to subdue the Jews. The Arabs took the city in A.D. 640. The Crusaders recaptured the city in A.D. 1002. In the centuries to follow, the city faded in influence and died.

Caesarea was a harbor city. A great levee with a tower on the end reached far out into the sea to protect the harbor which opened to the north. The levee was necessary to shelter the harbor from the sand-bearing currents sweeping up from Egypt. Otherwise any harbor along this coast quickly silts up. When the city declined and the levee fell into disrepair, the sands of time began to drift over Caesarea. Today vast sand dunes cover the ruins of what was one of the most illustrious cities of Palestine of Jesus' day!

Caesarea was a cosmopolitan city with a high development of Greek culture. A large Syrian population, many Jews, and a large colony of Romans lived here. Just prior to A.D. 66 there was a rebellion in Caesarea in which Syrians massacred a number of Jews. This was the beginning of the strife that spread throughout Palestine and eventually resulted in the Roman army marching in force to quell the rebellion of the Jews. This led ultimately to the destruction of the Temple and Jerusalem by Titus in A.D. 70.

The restored amphitheatre at Caesarea

The Pilate Stone, discovered in the amp theatre

Byzantine ruins of Caesarea

At Caesarea an aqueduct built in the f century by Herod

Caesarea plays a highly important role in the book of Acts. Philip (the evangelist and deacon), who had "four daughters who did prophesy," made his home here (Acts 8:4). Here Philip entertained Paul and his companions (Acts 9:30; 21:8).

Cornelius, a captain of the Italian brigade (or palace guard) lived at Caesarea. Peter came to his house from Joppa to preach the gospel for the first time to the Gentiles (Acts 10).

Paul landed at Caesarea several times during his missionary journey (Acts 18:22; 21:8). After Paul's arrest in Jerusalem, he was brought overnight to Antipatris, and then here to Caesarea. Here in Caesarea Paul was brought to trial before Felix (Acts 23:23-33); was imprisoned here for two years (Acts 24:27); and here Paul made his defense before Festus and Agrippa (Acts 25:26). Luke was with Paul during his imprisonment at Caesarea and some authorities believe that Paul wrote several of his epistles during this imprisonment.

Caesarea eventually became a Christian town. Origen was born here (A.D. 195). Eusebius, historian of the early church was born here (A.D. 260). Caesarea was a center of influence for early Christianity and a bishop was stationed here until A.D. 450. The city continued to play a prominent part in Muslim and Crusader history.

Excavations of the *Roman ruins* have revealed Caesarea to be a sumptuous city, skillfully engineered and magnificently adorned with columned buildings and statuary. In addition to the stone breakwater which created the crescent-shaped harbor, there was an elaborate and remarkably effective drainage system that carried off the water from this low-lying coastal location. The engineering of the drainage system is still considered a remarkable feat today.

Excavations have uncovered an ancient hippodrome with swimming pools and facilities for all kinds of sporting events, including chariot racing. A magnificent amphitheatre has been excavated and restored. It is used today for outdoor summer concerts. In the amphitheatre was found the famous "Pilate stone," a flat stone bench-seat engraved with the name of Pilate. This was Governor Pilate's "reserved seat" at the theatre! Pontius Pilate occupied the governor's residence at Caesarea, administering the affairs of his province from here and making excursions to Jerusalem only when administrative affairs required his presence. The discovery of this stone is but another confirmation from secular sources of the accuracy of the biblical record.

Excavations have also been conducted at the site of *Byzantine Caesarea.* Here is a courtyard dated several centuries after the Roman Caesarea of the New Testament era. An Italian marble floor with a beautiful mosaic has been uncovered. In the courtyard are two huge statues salvaged from the Roman era and erected here in the courtyard by the Byzantines. The dark porphyry torso is of the Emperor Hadrian, the white marble statue is of Zeus.

Other excavations are of Caesarea of the *Crusader Era.*

Jutting out into the sea is a Crusader mole, in which many porphyry and marble columns from the earlier ruins have been reused in the construction. On the mole are the remains of a Crusader fortress. Standing nearby are two well-preserved aqueducts, a high-level one built by Herod and a low-level aqueduct of a later date. These aqueducts brought water for human consumption and irrigation from the distant Carmel range down to Caesarea. The magnificent bastioned city walls and the restored gateway are of the Crusader period.

Caesarea in a unique way is connected directly with the missionary expansion of the gospel to all the people throughout the world. First, it was the home of Philip who preached the gospel to the Samaritans. Then Peter came here to preach the gospel to the Gentiles of Cornelius' household.

But here in Caesarea as perhaps nowhere else in the Holy Land you come under the giant shadow of the great missionary Paul.

Here at Caesarea the example of Paul's total commitment to the gospel and his words take on new meaning in our lives. "I have fought a good fight, I have finished my course, I have kept the faith: henceforth there is laid up for me a crown of righteousness, which the Lord, the righteous judge, shall give me at that day: and not to me only, but unto all them also that love his appearing" (2 Tim. 4:7-8).

6

Through Samaria to Galilee

Today you visit Samaria and Galilee.

Going north out of Jerusalem toward Nablus you pass through *Nob* (biblical *Shafat* where the tabernacle rested in Saul's day, 1 Sam. 21:1).

A lowlying hill on the right is *Gibeah* (Tel-e-Ful) Saul's birthplace and capital (1 Sam. 10:26). When the residents committed an inhuman crime against the concubine of a Levite, Israel marched against the city and slew practically all the Benjaminites who inhabited the city (Judg. 19-20).

The seven sons of Saul were hanged at Gibeah (2 Sam. 21:6-9). Excavations of the tel have uncovered four fortresses, each resting on the other, dating back to the time of the Judges.

Three miles out of Jerusalem you cross the old road to *Emmaus,* a village to the west. Somewhere along this road Jesus appeared to two disciples after the resurrection and ate in the house of Cleophus (Luke 24:13-31). Stones of the original Roman road rutted by the wear of chariot wheels can still be seen along the Emmaus road.

A short distance to the west of the highway is El-Jib, *Gibeon* of the Old Testament. It was a fortress city guarding the Valley of Ajalon which stretched further on to the west.

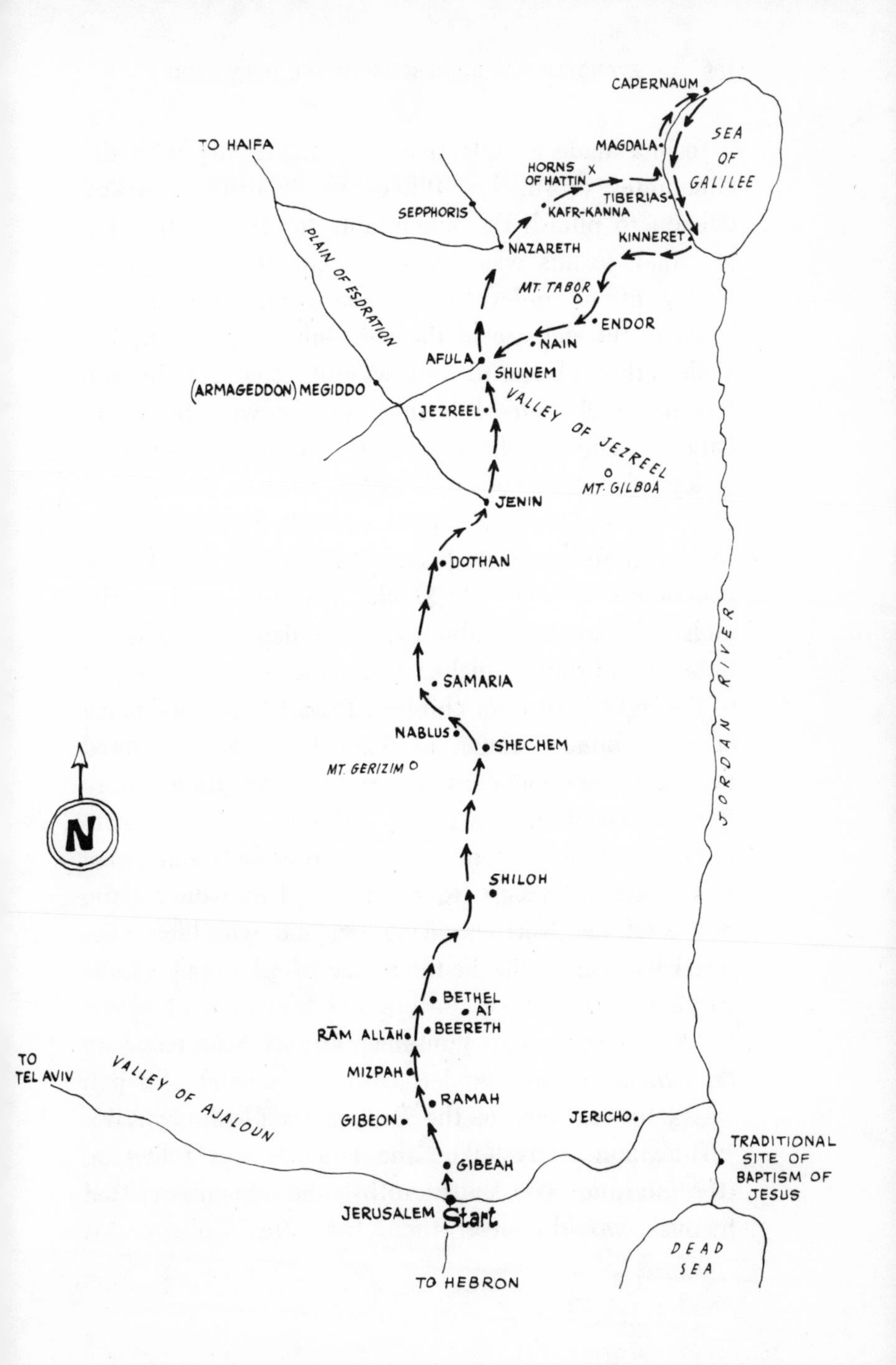
CAPERNAUM
SEA OF GALILEE
MAGDALA
TO HAIFA
HORNS OF HATTIN
TIBERIAS
SEPPHORIS
KAFR-KANNA
KINNERET
NAZARETH
PLAIN OF ESDRATION
MT. TABOR
ENDOR
NAIN
AFULA
SHUNEM
(ARMAGEDDON) MEGIDDO
JEZREEL
VALLEY OF JEZREEL
MT. GILBOA
JENIN
DOTHAN
SAMARIA
NABLUS
SHECHEM
MT. GERIZIM
JORDAN RIVER
N
SHILOH
BETHEL
AI
RĀM ALLĀH
BEERETH
TO TEL AVIV
VALLEY OF AJALOUN
MIZPAH
RAMAH
GIBEON
JERICHO
TRADITIONAL SITE OF BAPTISM OF JESUS
GIBEAH
JERUSALEM
Start
DEAD SEA
TO HEBRON

Joshua made a protective assistance treaty with the Gibeonites (Josh. 9). When the Amorites attacked Gibeon to punish the inhabitants for their subjection to Israel, Joshua was camped at Gilgal in the Jordan Valley fifteen miles to the east from here. Joshua came to the defense of the Gibeonites, up the Jordan Valley, through the pass by way of Ai, across through this area and routed the Amorites who were besieging Gibeon. The Israelites drove the Amorites down the valley of Ajalon far to the west clear to the coastal plains (Josh. 10). As the Amorites fled pellmell with Joshua in full pursuit, Joshua cried, "Sun, stand thou still before Gibeon . . . so the sun stood still in the midst of heaven . . . about a whole day" (v. 13).

A short distance further north, the town on the hill to the right is El-Ram (biblical *Ramah*) the birthplace of the prophet Samuel (1 Sam. 1:9). Samuel lived here and functioned as a circuit judge, traveling to Bethel, Gilgal, and Mizpah, judging Israel (1 Sam. 7:16-17). Ramah stood on the border between Israel and Judah. It was a heavily fortified city during the period of the Northern Kingdom and was later captured by Asa of the Southern Kingdom (1 Kings 15: 16-24).

After passing the Jerusalem airport you come to *Mizpah,* a hill on your left (Tel-en-Nasbeh). Mizpah was a fortress city of the Benjamites (Josh. 18:26).

Here Samuel resbuked the Israelites for following "the strange gods Ashtoroth" and promised that Jehovah would deliver them from the Philistines if they returned to him. When the Israelites were victorious, Samuel erected a stone and "called the name of it Ebenezer, saying, 'Hitherto hath the Lord helped us'" (1 Sam. 7). The phrase of the song, "Here I raise mine Ebenezer" is a reference to that event.

At Mizpah Samuel anointed Saul king and the people shouted "God save the king" (1 Sam. 10:24). During the period of the kingdom Mizpah was the scene of bitter fighting between Israel and Judah. Asa of Judah (913-873 B.C.) heavily fortified the city (1 Kings 15:16-22).

When this eight-acre tel was excavated, a town wall of the Judges-Kingdom period of Israel was uncovered. The wall is fifteen to twenty feet thick, in some places twenty-five feet high and could have been forty feet originally. In the wall is a city gate facing toward Bethel. By the gate is a sheltered area providing a seat of authority with long stone benches to the side where the town elders sat. Undoubtedly Samuel sat here judging and preaching to Israel as he held court at the city gate.

Nine miles out of Jerusalem you come to the modern cities of *Ramala* and *Bira*. The hill to the right is probably the site of *Beeroth,* one of the cities of the Hivite league (Josh. 9) which along with Gibeon tricked Joshua into making a mutual protection pact.

These people appeared at the camp of Joshua in Gilgal wearing old garments and wornout shoes and carrying sacks of moldy bread. They said: "We have heard how the God of Israel has delivered all the people into your hands, and we seek peace." The elders of Israel warned Joshua that God had commanded them to make no agreements with the people of the land. But the visitors pleaded, "We are not of this land. The clothes that are now tattered were once new. The bread that came hot out of the oven is now moldy. The shoes that are worn were once new. It is obvious that we have been on a very long journey." So Joshua was deceived and made peace with them only to discover that they came from nearby Beeroth and Gibeon.

The Israelites did not go to war against these cities but Joshua decreed that the people of Beeroth and Gibeon become "hewers of wood and drawers of water" thereafter. Excavations in this area have revealed large cisterns and water storage areas!

Beeroth was also the home of the two traitorous captains who slew Saul's son, Ishbosheth. (2 Sam. 4: 2). David avenged the treachery by commanding his young men to slay the two soldiers, cut off their hands and feet and hang them over the pool at Hebron. David buried the head of Saul's son with dignity in the sepulcher of Abner in Hebron (1 Sam. 4).

Excavations have revealed that this site was an ancient camping spot with abundant springs about one day's walking journey from Jerusalem. There is a tradition that the family of Jesus stopped here on their return from the temple only to discover that the boy was not with them. They went back the next day to find Jesus in the temple (Luke 2:43-52).

As you continue northward in the hills to the right are two very important Old Testament sites, *Bethel* and *Ai*.

Beitin is the modern name for the ancient site of *Bethel*. When Abraham first came from Ur of Chaldees, he dwelt here and built an altar (Gen. 12:8).

Here Jacob spent his first night as he fled from the wrath of his brother Esau, after stealing the birthright. Jacob saw in a dream "angels ascending and descending a ladder," made a covenant with God and called the place "Bethel—the house of God" (Gen. 28). Many years later he returned to Bethel to renew his vows (Gen. 35).

After the division of the kingdom in 920 B.C., Jeroboam, leader of the Northern tribes, erected an altar and a golden calf at Bethel. He told the people, "Do not go all the way up to Jerusalem. It is more convenient to worship Jehovah here!" And the people followed after idols! (1 Kings 12:25-33). The prophet Amos came out of the wilderness beyond to denounce this idolatry.

Two miles southwest of Bethel is the mound of *Ai*. As Joshua came up from the Jordan Valley through this pass into the highlands, Jericho was the fortress city guarding the mouth of the valley and Ai was the citadel at the head of the valley (Josh. 7-8).

At Ai the armies of Joshua met their first defeat. Then Joshua discovered that the defeat was due to the sin of Achan, a soldier who had disobeyed God and had hidden a wedge of gold in his tent. When the camp was made rid of the sin of Achan, the Israelites again marched against Ai and took the city.

From here the highway enters a broad valley and then rises on to a plain. On the right are the ruins of *Shiloh,* ancient Israel's sanctuary. After the main phase of the conquest of Canaan, Joshua brought the Israelites to Shiloh and cast lots for the division of the territory (Josh. 18:1 ff). Shiloh was the resting place of the ark of the covenant (1 Sam. 3:3-21).

Near Shiloh the Philistines and the Israelites were drawn up in battle array. When the Israelites brought the ark of the covenant from Shiloh into the camp, the Philistines said, "Let us capture the Ark of the Covenant and destroy this power of God that protects the Israelites." They launched an attack, captured the ark and the Israelites suffered a bitter defeat!

There was great wailing in Shiloh when the report came that the army had been defeated and the two sons of Eli the priest-judge had been killed. Eli, stunned by the news, fell backwards from his seat at the city gate and his neck was broken. His daughter-in-law, Phinehas' wife, was heavy with child. When she heard the bad tidings that the ark had been captured, her husband killed, and her father-in-law dead, she travailed in labor pains and died in childbirth. Still conscious when her son was born, she named the child, "Ichabod" meaning "The glory is departed from Israel."

Here at Shiloh during the wine festival remnants of

the Benjamites hid in the vineyards and captured for marriage the comely Shiloh girls who danced among the vines (Judg. 21:15-24). Here the Lord revealed himself to Samuel as a boy while he served the priest Eli (1 Sam. 3).

Shiloh was destroyed by the Philistines about 1050 B.C. Jeremiah refers to that destruction and excavations indicate that Shiloh was destroyed even as Jeremiah said.

Jacob's Well

Your first stop is in the Arab town of Nablus (the earlier name Neopolis). Near here is *Shechem* of biblical days, Abraham's first stop in Canaan where he built an altar (Gen. 12:6-7). Here Jacob bought a plot of land (Gen. 33:18-19) and Joseph tended his flocks (Gen. 37:12). Here Jacob's daughter was defiled (Gen. 34).

Here is located Jacob's well. This is an authentic site, where Jesus met the Samaritan woman (John 4). Wearied from his journey, and waiting by the well for the disciples to return from the village with food, Jesus asked the Samaritan woman for a drink and promised her "living water."

Perceiving he was a religious teacher, she asked which was the true abode of the Living God, the Temple of the Jews or of the Samaritans? Jesus answered that God is a spirit and he abides wherever men worship him in spirit and truth. During the conversation that followed, the much married Samaritan woman was converted and went back into her village telling her friends what had happened! To fully appreciate that situation you must understand the historical and geographical setting.

Genesis 22 tells of Abraham preparing to sacrifice his son Isaac to God in the "land of *Moriah*" (v. 2). *Moriah* is the mountain of Jerusalem where the Temple of the Jews was located (the Dome of the Rock today). However, not far from this location is the plain of *Moreh* which, except for the vowels, could be mistaken for Moriah. The Samaritan believed that it was to a hill near Moreh that Abraham brought Isaac. Facing Jacob's well across the road is *Mt. Gerizim,* a mount near the *Plain of Moreh* and here the Samaritans built their holy temple.

Both Jew and Samaritan believed that their temple alone was the true abiding place of God. This prompted the question of the Samaritan woman and the teaching of Jesus concerning the universal spirituality of the nature of God.

This is the original Jacob's well of Jesus' day. The ancient stone well-curb is covered today by an unfinished Russian Orthodox Church (a fourth-century Byzantine church once stood on this site). The debris of the centuries have filled in above the well. Going down a short flight of steps you come to the very curbstones where Jesus sat and talked with this Samaritan woman. The shaft is still "deep" (John 4:11), more than 150 feet deep.

Opposite Mt. Gerizim is Mt. Ebal. At the head of

"Where Jesus walked"—the rolling Palestinian countryside

A trench excavated at the Mound of Megiddo—the Valley of Jezreel in the distance

Camels of the dromedary variety—"ships of the desert"

The ruins of a Second-century synagogue at Capernaum

the valley on the slopes of Ebal is the little Arab town of *Askar,* identified as *Sychar,* the home of the Samaritan woman.

Shechem (near Nablus) was a powerful fortress Canaanite city as early as 2,000 B.C. The city guarded this heavily traveled road through the pass between the two mountains, Gerizim on the left and Ebal on the right.

After the completion of the southern campaign and the capture of Jericho and Ai, Joshua brought the tribes here to Shechem, built an altar on Ebal and erected a stone inscribed with the law (Josh. 8:31 ff). Half of the people gathered on Gerizim and half on Ebal. Just beyond the city of Nablus in the pass between the two mountains are two natural amphitheatres on the mountainside facing each other. It is here that the dramatic reciting of the blessings and the curses of the law took place (Josh. 24). Joshua recited all the things that God had done for the children of Israel and then said, "As for me and my house, we will serve the Lord."

Near Jacob's well in Nablus is a *Samaritan synagogue* and colony of approximately 300 Samaritans. The Samaritans were a hybrid people that originated during the time of the Babylonian captivity.

When the Northern Kingdom (Samaria) fell to the Assyrians under Sargon II (Sargon the Great) in 721 B.C., most of the Israelites were deported and settlers were brought in from Syria and the Upper Euphrates. Those who remained behind intermarried with these imported people and fell away from the Lord (2 Kings 17).

During the captivity ten tribes were lost in exile. Only Judah (hence the word Jew) and a portion of Benjamin returned in 537 B.C. to rebuild Jerusalem and the Temple. The Samaritans (the name given the hybrid Jews who had remained in the land) offered to help in the rebuilding of the temple. But the pure-blooded repatriated Jews would have no dealings with their mongrelized brethren.

The Samaritans tried to prevent the rebuilding of the Jewish Temple by flinging dead bodies into it at night thus making it ceremonially unclean according to Mosaic law. But in spite of this harassment the Temple was rebuilt in Jerusalem. The Samaritans later built their own temple here on Gerizim in 332 B.C. It was destroyed by John Hyrcanus in 128 B.C. and was never rebuilt.

The Samaritans do not accept any of the writings of the Jews beyond the book of Joshua. They still practice blood sacrifice at an altar on Mt. Gerizim and still observe the Passover according to the rules set forth in the Old Testament.

Samaria (Sebaste)

Five miles northwest of Nablus is a massive hill atop which are the ruins of ancient *Samaria* (Sebaste). If time permits, you will find a visit to these impressive ruins quite interesting.

This easily defensible site overlooking the chief

north-south trade route through the hill country was occupied as early as 3,000 B.C. Here Omri (the father of the weak king Ahab) founded the city of Samaria in 876 B.C. Samaria later became the capital of the Northern Kingdom (1 Kings 16:29). Elisha lived at Samaria for awhile, and Naaman the Syrian leper visited him and received instructions to bathe seven times in the Jordan to be healed (2 Kings 5:3 ff).

In 721 B.C. Sargon II captured and burned the city (2 Kings 17:5-6). Alexander the Great conquered Samaria in 331 B.C. Herod the Great restored Samaria in 27 B.C. and renamed it Sebaste, the Greek equivalent of the Roman name "Augustus."

Christianity came to Samaria when the deacon Philip preached the gospel to the Samaritans with great results (Acts 8).

Samaria, located on this high hill was one of the strongest citadel fortresses in the ancient world. There are several accounts of the besieging of Samaria. One siege lasted for three years (2 Kings 17:5). During the siege of Samaria by Benhadad, king of Syria, there is the gruesome story of the mother who ate the flesh of her child (2 Kings 6:24-33).

Excavations of this area have uncovered a Roman city of about A.D. 200, a rectangular columned forum, a covered portico, a basilica, the hippodrome, and the theater.

The finely constructed circular tower is from the Hellenistic period. In the fourth century B.C. Alexander the Great took Samaria. In rebuilding the city, he

At Jacob's Well—a Christian pilgrim leads a group in singing, "Fill My Cup, Lord."

imported skilled Macedonian stonemasons. This tower is an excellent example of their refined masonry construction which is quite superior to the crude workmanship of the native artisans.

Beyond this area, pieces of ivory (more than five hundred fragments) from inlays, panels, furniture, have been found giving evidence to the existence and location of the ivory palace of Ahab (1 Kings 22:39; Amos 6:5).

On the crest of the hill are the steps to the great temple of Augustus built by Herod the Great. Standing on these steps and looking to the west on a clear day you can easily see the Mediterranean Sea. On the coast twenty miles from here is Caesarea, the seat of the Roman government. Herod built this temple to the emperor Augustus on the summit of Samaria, with its gleaming white facade facing the Mediterranean so as to be clearly visible from Caesarea. Thus he shrewdly made vividly evident to the Roman authorities in the capital not only his building prowess but also his loyalty to the emperor!

Around the hill behind Herod's temple are the ruins of the Omri-Ahab period. Ahab was brought back to Samaria and died here and the blood in his chariot was "washed in the pool" at Samaria (1 Kings 22:38). Excavations have revealed a large pool in this area.

This finely constructed wall of the Omri-Ahab city goes back to the ninth century B.C. and is of special significance. The Israelites were a nomadic people, unskilled in urban crafts. So when they settled in cities, they were dependent upon the skills of other craftsmen.

Solomon was the first to import Phoenician masons and carpenters to work on the temple. This wall of Ahab's period is evidence that he also imported masons from Phoenicia. (His wife, Jezebel, was from the Phoenician city of Tyre.) So, in this wall we have an example of the type of masonry of the Temple of Solomon. Note the marginal drafting on two sides, that is, after the stone was first cut, it was shaped (or drafted) on the bottom and one side to fit the stones already set.

Six centuries later Herod the Great developed a work force of skilled masons and introduced another style of construction, stones with marginal drafting on all four sides, as seen here and in all other Herodian construction.

On the back side of the hill are the remains of the "Church of the Invention of the Head of John the Baptist." If you are to believe all the traditions, John the Baptist must have been quite active *after* his death. The Muslims claim that his *head* is in the mosque in Damascus. It is claimed that his *body* is buried in another location! Yet *another head* is buried here! (Some guides facetiously explain that in Damascus is "the head of John when he was a young man.") Yet, Josephus records that John was actually executed many miles from here, at Machaerus, a fortress overlooking the Dead Sea on the east side of Jordan.

Here an eleventh-century Crusader church was built

over the remains of a Byzantine church. A flight of steps leads down to a small chapel where a frescoe on the wall portrays the beheading of John the Baptist. The lower part of the frescoe shows the discovery of John's head. The church was built by the Crusaders on this site based on the fact that Herod's palace once stood here. However, these zealous early pilgrims mistook Herod the Great for Herod Antipas (who was responsible for the beheading of John the Baptist). Thus they "invented" the tradition that John was beheaded here at Samaria.

Thirteen miles north of Samaria the highway passes a low tel on the right, the site of ancient *Dothan*. Excavations have revealed a city located here as early as 3,000 B.C. (early Bronze).

Dothan was on the main caravan route from Damascus to Egypt. Here Joseph was seized by his jealous brothers, thrown into a well and later sold into slavery to the Midianites. Cistern pits like the one into which Joseph was tossed are still found in this area today. Camel caravans still make their way along the ancient trade route through this Dothan valley.

Elisha was at Dothan when the Syrians encompassed the town. In a vision Elisha saw the hills filled with "chariots of fire," defending the city (1 Kings 6:13 ff). The Lord struck the enemy with blindness and delivered Dothan as Elisha prophesied.

Five miles beyond Dothan is the Arab town of *Jenin* (ancient Engannim of Josh. 19:21) on the eastern edge of the great plain of Esdraelon and the Valley of

Jezreel. There is a tradition that Jesus cured the ten lepers here.

Continuing north from Jenin toward Nazareth, you pass the Arab village of *Yizre-el* on the right, site of ancient *Jezreel.* Here Ahab built a palace and Jezebel, his pagan wife, had Naboth stoned because he refused to sell his vineyard to Ahab (1 Kings 21). Jezebel was thrown from the palace window to her death by Jehu (2 Kings 9:10-37). Ahab's seventy sons' heads were displayed at the gate of the city after their execution (2 Kings 19:1-11).

Beyond Jezreel on the right are the mountains of *Gilboa,* scene of Saul's last battle with the Philistines in which he and Jonathan were killed and David became king (2 Sam. 1:17-21).

Three miles further north to the left on the slopes of "Little Mount Hermon" is the site of *Shunem.* Here lived a "great woman" and her husband who kept a guestroom or "prophet's chamber" for the tired Elisha (2 Kings 4:8-37). Elisha restored her son to life after he died from heat prostration while accompanying his father in the field. In the distance on the right and to the north is Mt. Tabor, a traditional site of the transfiguration (Luke 9:28).

Galilee

This northern section of Palestine west of Jordan is *Galilee* meaning literally "circle of the Gentiles." Some Jews settled this section on their return from exile and quickly adopted the customs and practices of the in-

Mary's Well in Nazareth, the only free-flowing source of water for the town

habitants. In Christ's time Galilee was a well-defined Roman province over which Herod Antipas (4 B.C. to A.D. 39) ruled (Luke 23:5-7). Herod Antipas built Tiberias on the shores of Galilee as his capital city.

The people of Galilee were devotedly religious and made regular pilgrimages to Jerusalem. But the pure-blooded more strictly orthodox brother-Jews of Jerusalem tended to despise the Galileans. Jesus appealed to the people of Galilee who "heard him gladly" (Mark 12:37). From among the Galileans Jesus recruited his first disciples, Peter, Andrew, James, John, Bartholomew, Thomas, Thaddeus, and Simon the Zealot.

Josephus writes that in his day there were three million residents in Galilee and one million in Judea. In the time of Jesus, this was a very lush, productive, and wealthy section. The hills were wooded with vast olive groves and numerous little villages dotted the landscape.

Galilee in Jesus' day was a progressive country open to new ideas. In the mountain range of Carmel were three main passes. The first to the east was the pass through which Elijah fled after his contest with Baal. The second was at Megiddo through which runs the *Via Maris* or "the way of the sea." The third pass was at Jenin (through which you have come today).

Because of these highways the peoples, caravans, and conquerors of the world passed through Galilee to make it a cosmopolitan area ever exposed to new ideas and new cultures. The Galileans of Jesus' day spoke Greek. We assume that Jesus also spoke Greek when he was in this area. The disciples from this area had both a Greek and Hebrew name such as "Simon-Peter." Today Galilee is blessed with heavy rainfall in the wintertime and two crops a year are produced in this area.

Nazareth

Six miles further north is Nazareth, situated in a rim of hills on the southernmost slopes of the Lebanon Mountains. Nazareth was the home of Joseph and Mary. From here they journeyed eighty-five miles south to Bethlehem for the Roman census where Jesus was born (Luke 1-2).

The city of Nazareth was the boyhood home of Jesus

(Luke 2:4,51; Matt. 2:23). We know only of one occasion when Jesus came back to Nazareth during his ministry. Offered an opportunity to preach in the synagogue (Luke 4:16 ff) he unrolled the scroll of the Old Testament and read from Isaiah 61.

It was then he said, "A prophet is not without honor save in his own town." He made an appeal for the universal application of the "good news," citing the examples of two prophets from the Old Testament who witnessed to non-Israeli people. It was then that the people rose up in anger and threatened to throw him from the cliff to destruction (Luke 4:28 ff). On the outskirts of the city is the traditional site of the *mount of precipitation* where he was threatened with death by being pushed downhill and stoned as a blasphemer.

In this city of Nazareth is a stone fountain called *Mary's well.* Water is piped to the fountain from a spring above on the hillside. A church has been erected over the spring itself. Inside, at the altar you may look through the floor and see the water flowing out of the spring. This is undoubtedly an authentic site, a well that existed in the time of Jesus. Mary certainly must have come to this well to draw water and the boy Jesus would also have come to the well to drink. Other sites in Nazareth such as the *workshop of Joseph* and the *kitchen of the Virgin Mary* are traditional and symbolic and have no authenticating evidence to support their claims.

A short distance to the west of Nazareth on the road to Haifa is *Sepphoris.* Sepphoris was a very beautiful city and the capital of Herod Antipas until he built

Tiberias by the Sea of Galilee. It is significant to Bible students because a Jewish rebellion occurred at Sepphoris when Jesus was a ten-year-old boy. Hundreds of revolutionaries were crucified on the road between Nazareth and Sepphoris (A.D. 6). Jesus as an impressionable boy undoubtedly saw this gruesome spectacle of men twisting and dying in agony on roadside crosses. He and others of Galilee well knew what Jesus meant when he later said, "Take up thy cross and follow me." It was a willing commitment to death by the most horrible means for the sake of the gospel.

The road from Nazareth to Tiberias runs northeast through the mountains of Gilead. Four miles out on the right is *Kafr-Kanna,* commonly but erroneously identified as New Testament Cana where Jesus performed his first miracle of changing water to wine. The true Cana is some eight miles to the northwest from this site (John 2:1-11).

Eight miles beyond Kafr-Kanna on the left in the distance are two hills and a saddle called the *Horns of Hattin.* In Judges 4 is the account of Deborah the prophetess sending the armies of Israel to war against Sisera.

When God sent a hailstorm, the chariots of the Canaanites became stuck in the mud and the Israelites won the battle. But Sisera escaped and fled to the tent of a friend named Heber who was camped near here. That night, Jael, Heber's wife, drove a tentpeg through Sisera's temples as he was sleeping!

Here also in the shadows of the *Horns of Hattin* the Kurdish warrior Saladin, after twenty-two years of

ns of a third-century synogogue at
ernaum

Ancient olive press found at Capernaum

Capernaum details of a frieze from the
agogue

Archaic rotary millstones at Capernaum

fighting, finally defeated the Crusaders in A.D. 1187. This brought to an end the eighty-four-year-old Latin kingdom of Jerusalem. Later crusaders regained a portion of the Holy Land but the Crusader army never fully recovered from this decisive defeat.

Sea of Galilee

The twisting road suddenly breaks over the crest of a hill and the breathtaking view compels you to stop. Below you is the Sea of Galilee nestled like a giant cup of azure blue liquid in a rim of mountains.

Galilee (or sometimes called Tiberias or Gennesaret) is a pear-shaped lake eight miles wide and 15 miles long at its extremities, 680 feet below sea level, with a depth of 400 feet at its deepest point. The Jordan River pours in from the north (to the left) and empties out to the south. The water is fresh and very clear.

The waters of Galilee still abound with fish today. One particularly tasty fish is called "Peter's perch," so named because of a marked pouch under the mouth and referring to the fish with a coin in its mouth that Peter caught. Jesus used the coin as an object lesson saying, "Render unto Caesar the things that are Caesar's and unto God the things that are God's" (Matt. 17:24-27).

The Sea of Galilee was a resort area in Jesus' day as well as today. The warm sulphur springs on the outskirts of Tiberias are believed to possess medicinal and curative powers. At the time of Jesus, this popular health resort attracted a large number of sick people thus explaining the presence of so many who came to

Jesus for healing during his ministry here (Mark 1:32 f; 6:53-56).

The Sea of Galilee is subject to violent storms (Matt. 3:24). Powerful thermo-drafts are created by the high mountains encircling it. Frequently strong winds funnel through the mountain passes to sweep the sea with sudden storms. Here Jesus miraculously stilled the storm (Matt. 6:45-52) and on another occasion walked on the water (Matt. 14:22-34).

From this vantage point on a clear day you can see majestic snow-capped Mt. Hermon sixty miles in the distance above the tip of the lake to the left. (Mt. Hermon is thought by some authorities to be the site of Christ's transfiguration, Matt. 16:13).

Tiberias

On the shores of Galilee is the modern city of Tiberias established by Herod Antipas as the capital of Galilee in A.D. 20 and named in honor of his patron, Emperor Tiberius. Many buildings in Tiberias are constructed of black basalt, a stone of volcanic origin.

We have no record of Jesus visiting the city. However, Tiberias was a center of rabbinical learning and Jewish influence during the first and second centuries A.D. Here the Mishna, the oral law which formed the basis of the Talmud, was compiled.

Turning to the north along the shores of Galilee, you pass the site of *Magdala* (Matt. 15:39; Luke 8:22), home of Mary Magdalene, and the ruins of *Bethsaida*, home of Peter, Andrew, and Philip (John 1:44; 12:21). Here Jesus healed a blind man (Mark 8:22) and later denounced Bethsaida for its unbelief (Luke 10:13; Matt. 11:21). Jesus probably was not referring to the Jewish population which was composed largely of fishermen but to the pagan section of the city. Philip the Tetrarch had rebuilt the city and a large colony of Romans had gathered here.

Further around the Sea of Galilee is a natural amphitheater in a little cove. This is probably the spot where Jesus gathered the crowd on the seashore and then withdrew in a boat to teach them.

Tabgha

Just beyond this cove is Tabgha, since Byzantine times identified as the site where the miracle of the loaves and fishes and the feeding of the five thousand took place (Mark 6:45; Luke 9:10). A church was first erected here in the fourth century. The well-preserved fifth-century mosaics of birds and fauna in the floor are some of the finest to be found in the Holy Land. A more recent mosaic commemorating the miracle of the loaves and fishes is at the altar.

The hill above and beyond this site on the left is the traditional *Mount of the Beatitudes* where some believe Jesus delivered the Sermon on the Mount. A beautiful thirteenth-century chapel is on the crest (Matt. 5 ff.).

Capernaum

Continuing a mile further along the northwestern shore you come to the ruins of Capernaum, a strategic city at the crossroads of several ancient trade routes.

Looking from the top of Masada toward a cinder cone below

The up-to-date seaport of Tel Aviv

A panoramic view of the coastline at Tel Aviv

Drinking from Jacob's Well at Samaria is an unforgettable experience.

Called "his own city" (Matt. 9:1), Capernaum was the operational center for much of the Galilean ministry of our Lord. Here he performed many healing miracles: the Roman centurion's servant, one sick of the palsy, one sick of an unclean spirit, Peter's mother-in-law of a fever (Matt. 8-9; Luke 4:33-36).

Here lived Matthew the tax collector (Matt. 9:9) and others whom he called as disciples (Matt. 4:13 ff). Here the disciples disputed over who would be the greatest in the kingdom (Matt. 9:33-37). Here a sympathetic Roman centurion gave the money to build a synagogue for the Jews (Luke 7:1-10). Here Jesus preached in this synagogue.

Extensive excavations by Franciscan fathers (begun in 1905) have revealed many relics that depict the everyday life of the people of Jesus' day. Found here are hour-glass-shaped millstones that rotated on a cone-shaped base. Grain poured into the top, worked downward as it was ground into flour that sifted out in a trough at the base. Also found here is an olive press and stone jars similar to those at the wedding feast at Cana where Jesus changed the water into wine.

The ruins of a third century A.D. synagogue have been excavated and partially restored by the Franciscans. After the destruction of Jerusalem in A.D. 70, great numbers of Jews moved into Galilee. In time this area became the center of Jewish culture and religious training while Judea declined in influence. This synagogue was built at the peak of Jewish affluence in Galilee. White limestone, imported from a distance, was used in construction rather than the common black basalt.

From the construction of the synagogue we can discern patterns of Jewish worship of that era. In the back of the synagogue is a balcony where the "high seats" for privileged persons were located. In Jesus' day the scrolls were kept in the north end of the synagogue at the back. But after the destruction of the Temple in Jerusalem, the scrolls were moved to the front. This and other changes in patterns of worship were for the express purpose of keeping continually before the people a visible reminder that the Temple had been destroyed and that Jews were to pray for its restoration.

Here in the synagogue are decorative friezes portraying various symbols of Judaism—the six-pointed star, the five-pointed star, the ark of the covenant in the desert as a small temple on wheels, the seven-branched candlestick, pomegranates, and grapes.

This synagogue had an outer court that may have been either the court for Gentile worship or a marketplace. In ancient times the marketplace was usually located beside the synagogue or the pagan temple in order that the people might conduct their commercial transactions as they came to worship.

Of particular Christian significance is the fact that this third-century synagogue appears to have been constructed on the site of an earlier synagogue (the one of Jesus' day, in which he taught). The earlier synagogue seems to have been built of the common black basalt stone, native to this area. The black foundation stones of that earlier synagogue are quite obvious at the base of this later structure. So, while we cannot say that Jesus actually taught in the synagogue that is now standing, we can assume that he probably stood on this very spot in the earlier synagogue teaching the people.

Excavations have also revealed what appears to be a channel cut from the sea up to the synagogue. This confirms the biblical account of the disciples getting in boats and coming to the synagogue. More recent excavations have uncovered a Byzantine church with a baptistery (providing for immersion) and fishermen's houses, one believed to be Peter's house where the healing of his mother-in-law took place (Matt. 8:5, 14-17).

Many dramatic events in the life of our Lord occurred within sight of these ruins at Capernaum. To the left, rising above the eastern shores of the Sea of Galilee, are the Golan Heights of Syria, ancient *Gadara,* where Jesus cured the demoniac and the swine ran into the sea (Mark 5:1-20).

It was in this synagogue that Jesus delivered the great message of John 6 (declaring himself the Bread of life). Then Jesus went around the edge of the lake to the wilderness and the crowds followed him. Late in the afternoon Jesus took the loaves and fishes of a lad and performed the miraculous breaking and multiplying of the food and fed the thousands.

In the evening, he went into the mountains to pray, and the disciples started across the sea in a boat.

When they encountered a storm, Jesus appeared to them in the darkness walking on the water, and delivered them. The following day the people sought Jesus, coming by boat until they found him. And he said unto them, "You do not seek me except for the bread and meat that I can give you."

As you stand at Capernaum and look out across the Sea of Galilee, these events and activities of our Lord become sharply vivid and dramatically real. And walking amid these ruins you realize the complete fulfillment of the prophecy of our Lord that Capernaum would be destroyed because of her unbelief (Matt. 11:23-24)!

The Jordan River

Two miles beyond Capernaum to the east the Jordan River enters the Sea of Galilee. But you are to visit the Jordan at its outlet. So you leave Capernaum retracing your route along the Galilean shore through Tiberias to Kinneret where the Jordan flows out to the south.

The Jordan River is mentioned often in the Bible in connection with many key figures: Lot selects the land he favors (Gen. 14:12-16); Jacob crosses Jordan (Gen. 32:10); Moses refers to Israel's crossing of Jordan (Deut. 3:20,25,27; Josh. 1:11 f; Ezek. 47:18); Gideon's victory over the Midianites (Judg. 7:24); Jepthah's dispute with Ammon (Judg. 11); David's flight and return over the Jordan (2 Sam. 10:17; 17: 22; 24; 19:15-39); Absalom's flight over the Jordan (2 Sam. 17:24); Naaman's healing of leprosy (2 Kings 5:10-14); Elijah crosses and ascends the Jordan (1

Kings 17:3-5; 2 Kings 2:6 ff); Elisha receives the mantle of Elijah (2 Kings 2:13-15); John the Baptist preaches and baptizes (Matt. 3:5; Mark 1:5; Luke 3:3); Jesus is baptized in Jordan (Matt. 3:13; Mark 1:9-11; Luke 3:21-22).

The word Jordan means "the river that rushes down." The river and valley are a part of the great Rift Valley, a rupture in the earth's crust extending five thousand miles from the Lebanon mountains across Palestine and into Africa. This sub-sea-level gorge is the deepest ditch in the world.

The Jordan Valley itself is one of the most unusual spots on the face of the earth—with the headwaters of the Jordan River in the foothills of Mount Hermon 1200 feet above sea level and its mouth emptying into the Dead Sea, the lowest spot on the face of the earth, 1286 feet below sea level. The valley is from 12 to 14 miles across, a very fertile area that is quite productive when irrigated. Through the center of the valley runs a twisting line of green, the trees and brush on the banks of the Jordan River, referred to in the Scriptures as the "jungle of the Jordan." Excavations have revealed that this valley once teemed with numerous prosperous villages.

The Jordan here at the outlet of the Sea of Galilee is very clear, but further below the waters are generally murky. Thus we can understand the Syrian Naaman's response to Elisha's command to wash in Jordan, "Are not the Abana and the Pharpar purer than the waters of the Jordan?" The average depth of the river is about five feet, with deeper holes along its course.

While the Jordan River is only 223 miles long, its significance is not in proportion to its size by any means! For here in the Jordan River our Lord was baptized. There are three traditional sites for his baptism. The strongest tradition favors a spot near the Dead Sea where the Allenby Bridge connects Israel with Jordan. While we cannot be absolutely certain of the exact spot of Jesus' baptism, this uncertainty does not mar our appreciation of this significant place. For the events were real. Along these very banks walked our Lord! Here John declared, "Behold, the Lamb of God that taketh away the sin of the world." And down into these very waters came our Lord to be baptized!

From the Jordan River you have the choice of two routes back to Jerusalem. The first is a new fast road down through the Jordan Valley to Jericho, and from thence into Jerusalem.

The second route adds one and one-half hours to your return time, but offers several additional sites of biblical interest. From Kinneret you may go twenty miles southwest to Afula, and then back to Jerusalem as you came, through Jenin and Nablus. Eight miles along the road to Afula on the right is *Mt. Tabor*. Opposite on the left is *Endor* where lived the witch who prophesied Saul's defeat in the fatal battle of Gilboa (1 Sam. 28:7-8). Six miles further on the left as you approach Afula is *Nain* where Jesus restored to life the son of a widow (Luke 7:11-15).

7

In the Land of the Philistines

Today you visit the land of the Philistines. On the new superhighway northwest from Jerusalem you quickly cover the thirty-five miles to Tel Aviv!

Tel Aviv

Tel Aviv, meaning "hill of spring," was founded by Jewish immigrants in 1909 in the suburbs of ancient Joppa. The growing city soon became a world center for Zionism and a symbol of the Jewish hope for the restoration of a national homeland. Today Tel Aviv is the cultural and economic center of Israel. Strolling through the ultra modern shopping district you feel the pulse beat and dynamics of the economy that the Jews have wrought in this semiarid nomadic and agricultural land!

Time permitting, several excellent museums are worth visiting (two of particular biblical interest). *The Hartz Museum* (on Ramat Abib) contains antiquities organized in sections of glass, ceramics, numismatics, and folklore. *The Museum of Antiquities* (Mifratz Shelomo St.) contains artifacts from the Neolithic to the Roman era.

Jaffa (Joppa)

Incorporated in Tel Aviv is modern-day Jaffa, the site of the ancient port city of Joppa (one of the

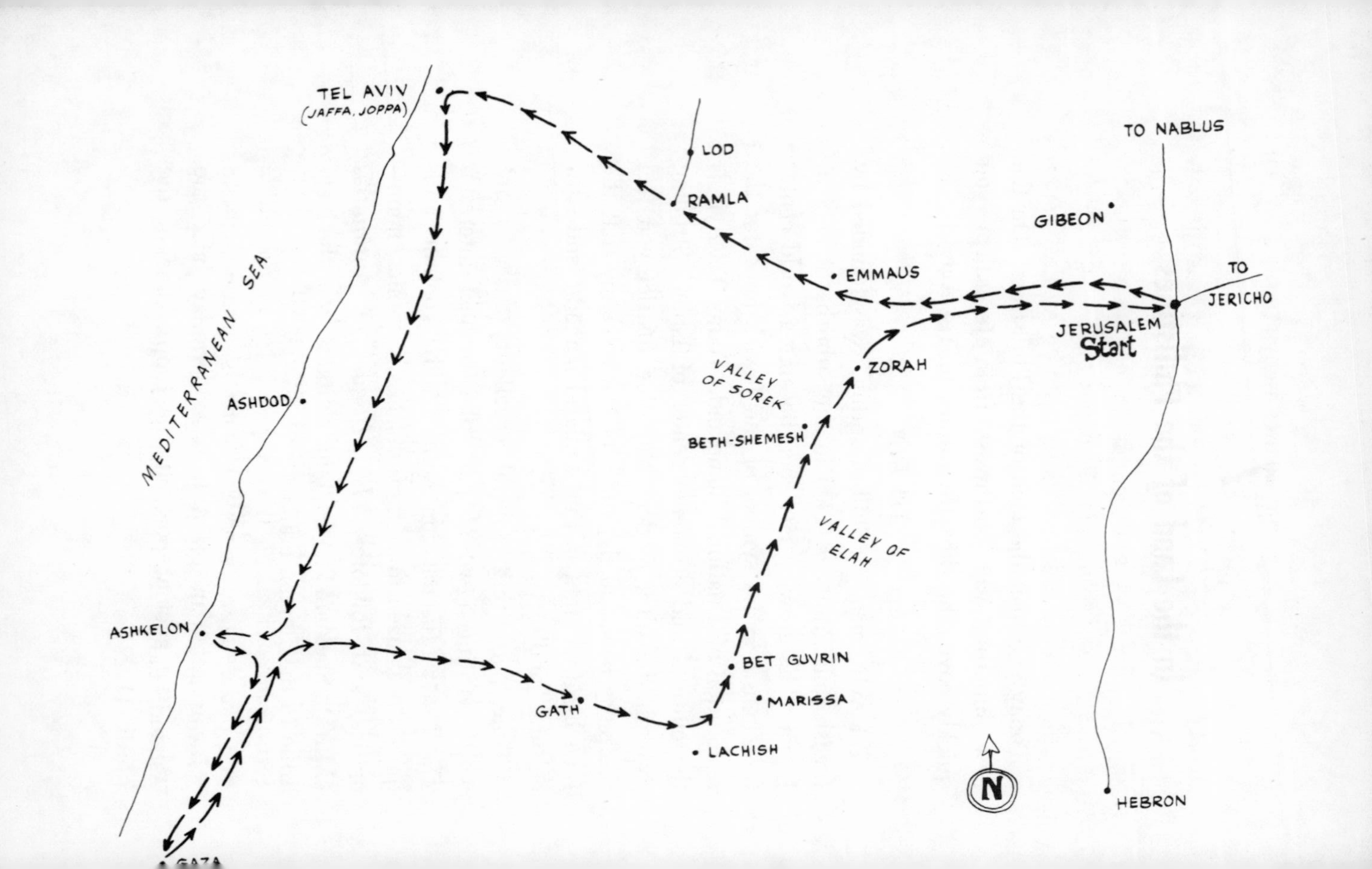
TEL AVIV
(JAFFA, JOPPA)
LOD
RAMLA
TO NABLUS
GIBEON
EMMAUS
TO
JERICHO
JERUSALEM
Start
MEDITERRANEAN SEA
ZORAH
VALLEY OF SOREK
ASHDOD
BETH-SHEMESH
VALLEY OF ELAH
ASHKELON
BET GUVRIN
GATH
MARISSA
LACHISH
N
HEBRON
GAZA

world's oldest cities). In biblical times it was the only harbor on the Mediterranean between Mt. Carmel and Egypt. Before the development of the present-day docks, cargoes from ships tendered in the harbor were brought ashore in heavy skiffs manned by the famous singing Joppa boatmen.

Jonah embarked from Joppa for Tarshish running away from the call of God to preach to Nineveh (Jonah 1:3,17). In the Old Testament period, Joppa was the northernmost city of the Philistines.

In the New Testament period, Peter had a significant ministry here. The faithful woman Dorcas sewed and labored for the Lord here. When she died, Peter raised her from the dead (Acts 9:36-42).

The home of Simon the Tanner was also in Joppa. Here on the rooftop Peter had the vision of "clean" and "unclean" food which led him to preach the gospel to the Roman centurion Cornelius in Caesarea (Acts 10). In Joppa today there is a traditional site of Simon's house. While there is little archaeological evidence to support this particular site, this is ancient Joppa, and somewhere in this immediate area Peter did receive his vision from the Lord.

Today ancient Joppa is being restored and developed as an artists' colony and tourist attraction.

From Joppa you travel south paralleling the Mediterranean coast along the western edge of the Philistine plain. Three miles south of the present city of *Ashdod* on a high hill to the right is the tel of ancient Ashdod, dating back to the sixteenth century B.C. (Josh. 11:22).

Ashdod was one of the five city-states of Philistia (the others, Askelon, Gaza, Gath, and Ekron). They were at their peak of influence and power during the Hebrew monarchy (1020-587 B.C.). Mentioned 21 times in the Old Testament Ashdod was one of the cities to which the Philistines brought the captured ark of the covenant. It was first placed in the temple of Dagon, resulting in disastrous afflictions on the Philistines. Then it was carried to Gath and Ekron with the same dire consequences. It was finally voluntarily returned to the Israelites. With a newly constructed port, the modern city of Ashdod is a major shipping point for Israel today.

Ashkelon

Seven miles further to the south is the modern seaside resort city of Ashkelon. The ruins of the ancient city are on its southern edge. Extensive excavations indicate a city existed here as early as the Canaanite period (2000 B.C.). Columns and foundation stones from pagan temples dating back to Samson's day have been uncovered. The Romans, the Arabs, and the Crusaders also left their mark on the city.

Amid the ruins are many statues of the Roman era with the facial features obliterated by the Muslim chisel during the Arab occupation. The Muslim religion forbids the reproduction of human features in art forms lest it appear as an expression of idolatry. A particular example is the beautiful Roman statue of the goddess of victory, holding a palm branch in her hand. The features have been completely defaced by the zealous Arabs.

The Crusaders built a fortress here. The bastion wall facing the Mediterranean incorporates ancient stone columns gathered from earlier ruins and laid parallel to reinforce the barricade. Erosion has cut away the smaller stones, leaving the columns protruding from the wall to give the appearance of huge cannon barrels guarding the silent ruins.

Here also is a six-hundred-year-old mechanized well that used donkey power. Philistines using iron-tired chariots occupied Ashkelon (Judg. 14:19). Zephaniah (2:4) and Zechariah (9:5) prophesied the destruction of Ashkelon. Herod the Great was born at Ashkelon and his sister Salome resided here.

Gaza

Time and political circumstances permitting, you may visit Gaza, twelve miles to the south of Ashkelon. Gaza was situated at the crossroads of the most important caravan routes of the ancient world. It was a major trading center of biblical Palestine. Even today modern Gaza is still a congested busy center with streets thronged by picturesque crowds. Gaza produced a light textile fabric that gave us the modern word "gauze."

First an important Egyptian city, Gaza was captured by the Philistines (Judg. 1:18; 6:4; 16) and became the principal city of the Philistine league.

Samson is credited with carrying off the gates of

the city of Gaza eastward toward Hebron (Judg. 15). Later at Gaza he was betrayed by his lover, Delilah, who cut his hair and turned him over to the Philistines who bound him, blinded him, and made him to grind in the prisonhouse. Later Samson pulled down the columns of the temple of Dagon (the God of Agriculture and chief deity of the Philistines) destroying himself and a great number of the leaders of Philistia (Judg. 16).

In modern times Gaza has been a pawn in the Israeli-Arab conflict. Before the Six Day War of 1967 the Gaza strip was tied to Egypt. Several hundred thousand Palestinian refugees were quartered there. In the Six Day War Israel occupied Gaza and the supervision of the teeming refugee camps passed into her hands.

From Gaza you return to Ashkelon and turn eastward across the Philistine countryside eleven miles to *Qiryat Gat.* Here on the left is the probable site of *Gath,* another of the Philistine city-states and home of the giant Goliath (1 Sam. 17:4-50).

Eight miles further on the right at *Bet Guvrin* is the tel of *Marissa* (Mareshah of the Old Testament). Here the Lord smote the "thousand thousand" Ethiopian invaders (2 Chron. 14:9-12) under King Asa of Judah. Extensive excavations have revealed the best preserved town of Hellenistic Palestine (third century B.C.) yet to be uncovered, providing a wealth of information about the religious ideas and the cultural patterns of this era.

Six miles further north the road crosses a little brook at the authentic site of the *Valley Elah.* The plains were held by the Philistines. The Israelites held the foothills to the north. The Philistines came up from the plains and took the first hill. The Israelites camped across the valley and the brook on the opposite hill. And here unfolded the famous drama when the shepherd boy David slew the Philistine giant Goliath with a pebble gathered from this brook (1 Sam. 7:17).

It was in this area that Samson released the foxes that set fire to the fields of Philistia (Judg. 15). Looking to the south and the east across these rolling plains, it is easy to imagine the chaos created by the fires of Samson.

Six miles further north the road passes through *Bethshemesh,* site of an ancient Canaanite town (Josh. 15:10; 1 Sam. 6; 2 Chron. 25:23; 28:18). The name means "the house of the sun," and was the center of Canaanite worship of the sun god.

After capturing the ark of the covenant in battle, the Philistines became frightened when their god fell face forward in the presence of the ark and Philistine soldiers died. They willingly returned the ark to the Israelites, and it rested at Bethshemesh (1 Sam. 6:9).

Beyond Bethshemesh to the left is *Zorah,* Samson's birthplace. It was near here that the spirit of the Lord came upon Samson and he killed a lion with bare hands (Judg. 14:5). Just beyond Zorah the road joins the Tel Aviv-Jerusalem highway. From here it is only a twenty-minute drive to Jerusalem.

8

Masada, Beersheba and the Bedouins

Today you visit *Masada,* Herod's fortress in the desert, the *Negev* and *Hebron.*

Traveling southeast from Jerusalem past Jericho and along the western shores of the Dead Sea, you pass the spring-fed tropical oasis of *Engeddi,* eighteen miles below Qumran. Excavations at this ancient site have revealed remains of human habitation and a pagan temple of 3500 B.C.! In a cave nearby David took refuge from Saul and also spared his life (1 Sam. 24). Other references are Ezekiel 47:10; Genesis 14:7; 2 Chronicles 20:2.

Today a *kibbutz* has been established at Engeddi. Throughout Israel you see these collective villages called kibbutz where people live in a communal pattern of life. This movement has been strongly influenced by the socialist philosophy which seeks to bring equality between men and women and between classes.

Participation in the kibbutz is voluntary. The members eat together, share together, and divide up the work of the farm. The children usually sleep, eat, and are reared separately in dormitories or special houses apart from the adults. Thus both parents are free to work and spend only a few hours daily with their children. The children are cared for by special nurses

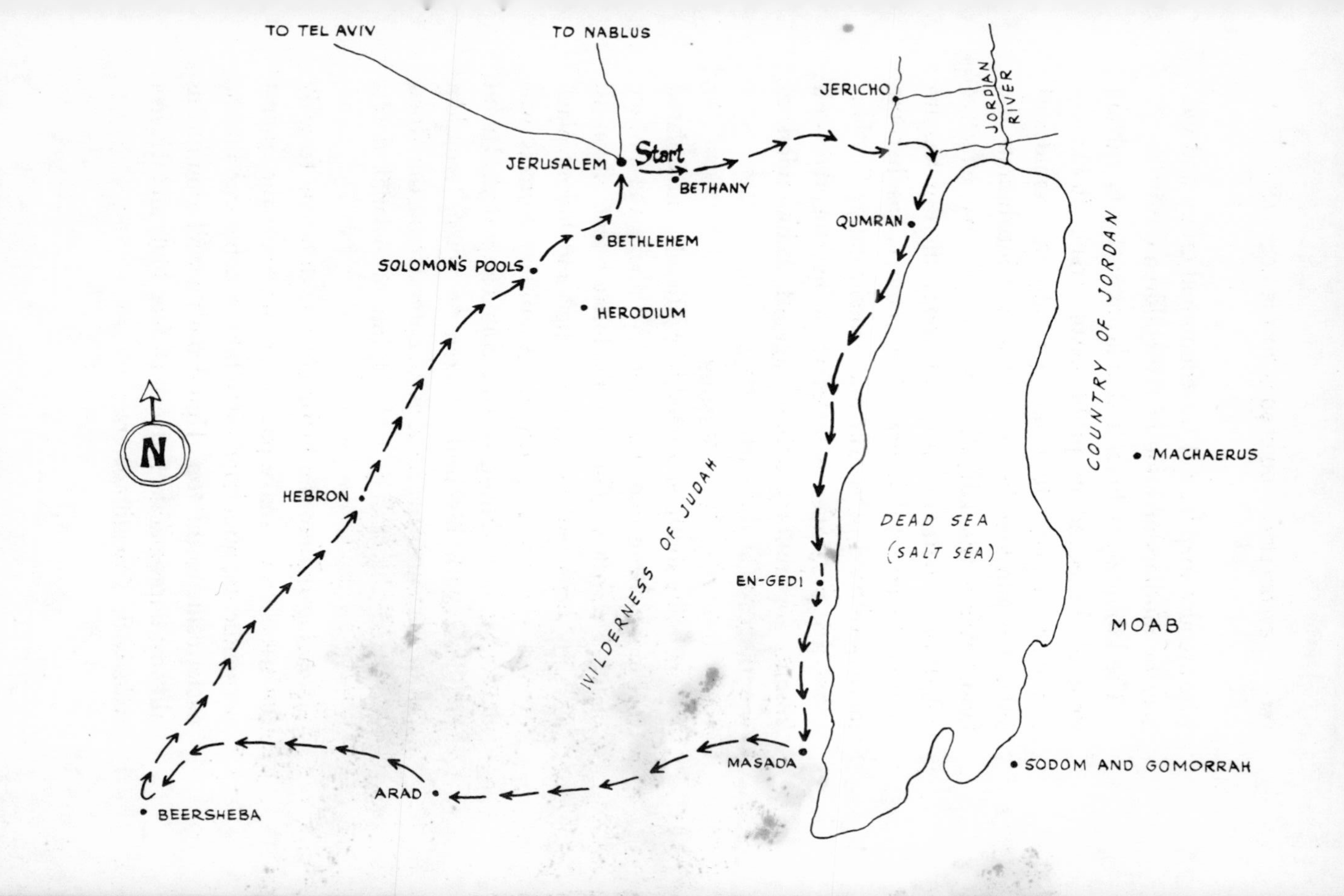
TO TEL AVIV
TO NABLUS
JERICHO
JORDAN RIVER
JERUSALEM
Start
BETHANY
QUMRAN
BETHLEHEM
SOLOMON'S POOLS
HERODIUM
COUNTRY OF JORDAN
N
MACHAERUS
HEBRON
WILDERNESS OF JUDAH
DEAD SEA
(SALT SEA)
EN-GEDI
MOAB
MASADA
SODOM AND GOMORRAH
ARAD
BEERSHEBA

who are also members of the communal group and who may be mothers of some of the children.

The kibbutz has been a significant factor in solving some of the economic problems of Israel. It has encouraged pioneers to come out into the semidesert areas and join together to reclaim and rehabilitate the land. While the kibbutz has been a very effective colonizing program in the past, today there is less incentive to join a kibbutz. The country has become more developed physically and economically. Furthermore, it is no longer as necessary to live together in a kibbutz for military defense against Arab raiders as was the case in the earlier days.

Masada

Ten miles south of Engeddi is Masada, an isolated rock peak rising one thousand feet above the surface of the Dead Sea. This natural fortress, cut off on all sides by keep valleys, was a refuge and hiding place even in the times of David. A military fortress was developed here during the interbiblical period. Herod fled here with his bride Mariamne when Jerusalem fell to the Parthians in 42 B.C. Later Herod the Great converted this lonely fortress into a palatial desert retreat.

Leaving the more athletic and venturesome to walk the treacherous snake-path that twists up the almost perpendicular precipice—you take a cable car up the eastern side to the top. Herod built a wall around this already impregnable fortress 18 feet high and 12 feet wide with 37 watchtowers.

An ancient Canaanite altar at Megiddo

Qumran with the Dead Sea in the distant background

The pock-marked face of Golgotha, often called Gordon's Calvary

The Samaritan Pentateuch, one of the few ancient scrolls not in a museum

On the western decline he erected a palace with three levels of living, complete with a throne room, residential quarters, terraces, and workrooms. He constructed barracks and storehouses for food and arms for a thousand soldiers. Aqueducts from the distant Judean hills fed water into the huge underground cisterns carved from the solid rock of Masada.

Public and private buildings were elaborately decorated with walls painted to imitate marble. The floors were paved with beautiful mosaics in geometric and floral designs. Here also was a synagogue with a pillared hall and benches around the wall set facing toward Jerusalem.

While there is no reference in the New Testament to Masada, these ruins do provide an excellent picture of the expansive and affluent construction of the great builder, Herod the Great. Masada was only one of several such fortress-prisons developed by Herod. (Machaerus, a similar rocky mountain peak on the other side of the Dead Sea was another such fortress and was the place where John the Baptist was beheaded.)

Masada is of special historical significance to the Jews. Here the Jewish nation made its last dramatic stand against Rome. In A.D. 66 a band of Zealots led by Manachen Ben Yehuda captured Masada from the Romans who had occupied the fortress since Herod's death. Thus began the great and final Jewish revolt against Rome. The Zealots' bold action had been triggered by the orders of the mad emperor Caligula who commanded that his statue be erected in the Temple in Jerusalem.

The revolt quickly spread throughout Palestine. Rome sent first Vespasian and then Titus to subdue the Jews, and Jerusalem fell in A.D. 70. But the Zealots continued to hold Masada against the Romans. In A.D. 72 the Roman general Silva marched from Jerusalem with his tenth legion to conquer Masada and crush the last remnant of Jewish resistance. Silva's army numbered 15,000 soldiers and captured Jews who were used as camp laborers. The Jewish defenders of Masada numbered 967 men, women, and children.

Silva besieged Masada in the fall of A.D. 72, circling the base with an impregnable ring of walls and eight Roman camps. But the Romans found it impossible to breach the upper wall by assault, even with this massive army of trained soldiers. The handful of Zealots easily repulsed them by throwing stones down on their heads.

Then the Romans adopted another strategy. Using Jewish slave labor, they began construction of an earthen ramp across the valley on the western side up to the fortress. The Zealots could not bring themselves to attack the laborers who were their blood brothers. They waited in silent and hopeless desperation atop the fortress as the earthen ramp was slowly formed by the thousands of Jewish slave laborers. When the ramp was completed, the Romans easily rolled huge siege engines and battering rams up the ramp to the fortress walls atop Masada. This final attack was in the spring of A.D. 73.

At last, the Zealots knew that the end had come. Their leader Eleazer called the men, women, and children together and made an eloquent plea, "We shall die before we become slaves to the enemy, and remain free as we leave the land of the living–we, our wives, and our children." So the group made the last terrible decision to die by their own hands rather than to live in slavery. Ten men were chosen by casting lots to determine who would slaughter all the rest. After all others had been executed, one among the ten would kill the other nine. When assured that he alone was alive, the last man would set fire to the palace, the food stores and supplies, and commit suicide on his own sword!

Thus Masada was destroyed and the Romans found a devastated city of the dead when they breached the wall the next morning. The Zealots all died believing that not a living soul had been left behind to carry the Roman yoke. However, three persons, two women and a child, hiding in a storeroom, were somehow overlooked and remained alive to tell the story to the Romans.

Today Masada is a national shrine for Israel, a singular symbol of national purpose and destiny. The new nation is surrounded by a hostile Arab world outnumbering them forty to one. Masada signifies the stand of a few against many, the weak against the strong. Masada symbolizes the fight of valiant Jews

An Arab farmer plows his field exactly as his forefathers did during biblical days.

An Arab family on the move with household belongings loaded on their "vehicles"

who gave up their lives for political and religious freedom, choosing rather to die than to submit to slavery! Masada is as an anvil on which the present generation of Israelis forge their history and destiny. Young men and women are brought here for induction into the army and to pledge that "Masada shall not fall again."

Beersheba

From Masada you go due west, passing through *Arad,* a new city of the desert offering excellent food and lodging accommodations. It is fifty miles to Beersheba in the Northern Negev. Near the present city are ancient ruins which go back six thousand years to the Chalcolithic period (a Greek word meaning copper-stone). It was in this era that metal objects of cast copper first appeared. The copper came from the mines of *Arava* in the Negev which are still productive today.

Abraham came to Beersheba and was the original owner of the wells that supplied water for the flocks (Gen. 21:22-31). An old well to the south of the city is still called "Abraham's well."

Beersheba continued to be a significant site and a favorite dwelling place of the nomadic patriarchs Abraham, Isaac, and Jacob (Gen. 28:10). "From Dan even to Beersheba" (Judg. 20:1) became a classic phrase to describe the north-south limits of Palestine.

Elijah fled to Beersheba from the wrath of Jezebel (1 Kings 19:3). The perpetual supply of water in and near the town has made it a key city of the southern section of Palestine even to this day.

Beersheba continues to this day to be a Bedouin trading center. At the weekly Thursday market you see Bedouins who still live in a culture little changed from biblical times.

Throughout Palestine you frequently see the tents of the Bedouins or shepherds with their herds. During the course of a day a shepherd will cover five to six miles with his flock. In farming areas there are no fences and the wandering herds are a threat to the crops. Consequently, the farmer himself, or an employee, must live in the fields during the growing season to protect the crops from the flocks of wandering Bedouins. The watchman lives on a little raised platform made of sticks or possibly a stone tower, a watchtower as referred to in the Scriptures.

It is possible for the Bedouin to live entirely off his herd. He gets milk, meat, wool for clothing, and goat hair for his tent materials from the herd.

A meal with a Bedouin family is an unforgettable experience. The dinner party sits in the tent in a circle, cross-legged on rugs spread on the sand. The meal begins with strong coffee. Then rice is eaten (by hand) out of a common bowl by rolling the rice in a ball and throwing it into the mouth. Meat is also eaten by hand off a common plate. The meal ends with a sweet tea. Supposedly the wealth of a Bedouin is indicated by the number of free-standing poles in his tent.

At the *Negev Museum* in Beersheba is an excellent collection of archaeological finds from all periods and an ethnological collection illustrating Bedouin life.

Traveling northeastward toward Jerusalem you come into rolling highlands three thousand feet above sea level covered with vineyards and olive groves. This is the region of *Eschol.* From this area the spies, sent out by Moses, brought back grapes hanging on a pole between two men (Num. 13:14-25). Israel's national insignia is a stylized form of two men carrying a huge bunch of grapes. This fertile land, green and rich in vineyards and groves must certainly have appeared as a land "flowing with milk and honey" to the children of Israel who had wandered so long in the desert wilderness!

Hebron

Thirty miles northeast of Beersheba is the huge Arab city of Hebron. Located on a natural highway from central Palestine into Egypt, Hebron (also called Kiriyat Arba) is mentioned many times in the Old Testament.

Hebron was Abraham's home during his sojourn in this area (Gen. 18). Here was the burial place of Abraham, Isaac, Jacob, Leah (Gen. 49:31; 50:13). The spies found the giant Anakim among Hebron's inhabitants (Num. 13:22). Joshua captured and destroyed the city during the conquest of Canaan (Josh. 10:39; 11:21-23).

David was anointed king at Hebron (2 Sam. 2:11).

Six of his seven sons were born here (2 Sam. 3:2-5). Absalom raised his standard of rebellion against his father David at Hebron (2 Sam. 15:10).

Hebron continues to this day to be a thriving trading center, famous for its handblown glass and pottery products.

Of particular biblical significance is the Muslim mosque erected over the Cave of Machpelah, the family burial site of the patriarchs. When Sarah died, Abraham asked the children of Heth, who dwelt in the land, for a burial place for his wife (Gen. 23). They replied that Abraham could have the site of his choice for "they would not withhold from him a sepulcher for his dead." So at the city gate of Hebron they asked Ephron the Hittite for the cave of Machpelah for Abraham. Excavations of ancient cities usually reveal benches around the gate where the people gathered to discuss the issues of the day and transact business. (See the comments on Shiloh.) So in the presence of the elders of Hebron at the city gates Abraham negotiated with Ephron.

In this story is the familiar pattern of Oriental bargaining. Ephron says, "Take what you will, the cave and the field as well, for you are a prince among the people." Abraham replied, "I shall be glad to pay."

After bargaining back and forth, the price was set at four hundred shekels of silver. A shekel was a weight of money, not a coin, since stamped coinage did not develop in this part of the world until about 500 B.C. (Although, there was a coin called a shekel in

Jesus' day.) So Abraham laid out the silver by weight and purchased this very site, the Cave of Machpelah, as a burial place for Sarah. Later Abraham, Rebecca, Jacob, and Leah were also buried here. Rachel, however, was buried to the north near Bethlehem.

This is undoubtedly an authentic site, the Cave of Machpelah over which the Muslim mosque is built. The exterior rectangular walls were first constructed by Herod and rebuilt and enlarged several times in the centuries to follow. Inside the walls is a vaulted Crusader church that has been converted into a mosque.

In the earlier Byzantine period a Christian church was built on the spot and subsequently destroyed. An earlier Muslim mosque had also been built here in the Arab period and was destroyed. In the exterior walls and along the passageway inside is seen the typical Herodian masonry with the marginal drafting on four sides.

This site is sacred to both Jew and Muslim as Abraham was the father of both peoples. In the pre-Israel days Arabs controlled the mosque. When Jews made pilgrimages to Hebron to this sacred shrine, the fifth step in the entryway was the furthest point that the Jew was allowed into the mosque. At the step was a small opening in the stones which connected with the cave below. Devout Jewish pilgrims would insert prayer petitions written on scrolls or pieces of paper in this hole to fall into the cage below. They believed that for their petitions to mingle with the bones of the patriarchs gave special efficacy to their prayers.

Plaster now covers the hole and since the Six Day War Jews may enter all the way into the mosque.

In earlier days other non-Muslims besides Jews were also excluded from the mosque and allowed to go only as far as the seventh step. The eighth step is a large stone twenty-five feet long and five feet wide, part of the Herodian construction.

In the outer area are the *cenotaphs* (or tombs) of Jacob and Leah. In the vestibule are the tombs of Abraham and Sarah. Further inside are the tombs of Isaac and Rebecca. The patriarch's tombs are covered with elaborate gold-embroidered green textiles and the women's tombs with crimson. Another tomb is said to be that of Joseph. However, the biblical account indicates that Joseph was buried at Shechem (Gen. 50:25-26; Josh. 24:32).

These tombs do not contain the bones of the patriarchs, but it is claimed that they rest directly over the actual spot in the cave below where the bones are found. We have no evidence to confirm these claims.

No one in recent times has inspected the cave. It was sealed at the time of the Crusaders and not even the most devout Muslim is allowed to enter the cave today. However, it is known that in 1917 when the British took this area from the Turks, the guards of the mosque fled and a colonel under General Allenby did enter the cave. He wandered about undisturbed, but did not explore the cave extensively.

There were three entrances to the Cave of Machpelah. Two have been completely blocked up.

Through a grating in the floor of the mosque, you may look through the third opening into the cave below.

As you leave Hebron to the north, on the right is the traditional site of the well of *Sirah* (2 Sam. 3:26) where Joab brought Abner to the gates of Hebron and slew him in revenge.

Two miles out of Hebron on the left is the purely traditional site of the *Oaks of Mamre*, the giant trees under which Abraham first pitched his tents (Gen. 13:18); where the angelic messengers announced to Abraham the birth of a son (Gen. 18:1-14); and where the Lord revealed to Abraham the destruction of Sodom and Gomorrah (Gen. 18:17 ff).

When Eurtrophia, the mother-in-law of Constantine, visited the Holy Land, she reported that a pagan Roman shrine had been erected on this location north of Hebron. Constantine wrote a letter to the bishop of Jerusalem (reported by the church historian Eusebius) expressing a desire that the pagan shrine be torn down and a Christian basilica erected here. The ruins of that church may be seen at the back side of the present enclosure. The wall itself dates to the time of Hadrian (second century A.D.). The site today is called "The Enclosure of the Hilltop of the Friend of God."

Continuing northward toward Jerusalem, two miles south of Bethlehem on the right are *Solomon's Pools* (Eccl. 2:6). However, these three reservoirs were probably built in the second century B.C. rather than by Solomon. In Roman times Pontius Pilate renovated them and repairs have kept them in operation.

Passing through Bethlehem you return to Jerusalem.

Israel Today

The state of Israel was proclaimed a republic May 14, 1948. The Parliament is a 120-member Knesset elected every four years. The government is headed by a prime minister.

Prior to June 1967 Israel covered an area of 8,000 square miles and it did not include the Negev and a large "bulge" of territory west of the Jordan. The population at that time was approximately 2.5 million Jews and a half million Arabs and others.

The Six Day War expanded Israel's borders eastward to the Jordan and all the way south to the Suez to include all the Sinaitic Peninsula. The geographical area was increased to 26,100 square miles and approximately 1.1 million additional Arabs were brought under the jurisdiction of Israel.

Today Hebrew, the revived language of the Bible, is the common language of Israel. Arabic is also widely spoken throughout the country.

The sabbath commences at sundown on Friday and ends at nightfall on Saturday. Government offices, public institutions, shops and most public transport ceases on the sabbath in the Jewish sections. However, Friday is the day of worship for the Muslims, and Arab shops in the Arab sectors are generally open on the sabbath.

Kosher is food prepared according to Jewish dietary laws. Kosher food is served in practically all of Israel's hotels and restaurants (other than those operated by Arabs in Arab sections). There is no difference in taste, but you will not be served cheese or milk with a meat dish. In practical application, this means "no cream with your coffee at a kosher meal if there is meat on the table."

The weather in Israel is subtropical. While the temperatures in the summer are somewhat higher than in the United States, the low humidity and the high altitude make summer most pleasant throughout the greater portion of Israel. The winter (the rainy season) is very mild, comparable to early fall in the Southern United States.

Travel Tips

Only a valid US passport is required for admission to Israel. There are no special shots or vaccinations required.

There is no need to convert dollars to Israeli pounds as US currency and travelers checks are readily accepted for all services and purchases in Israel. Many shops accept personal checks.

Wood carvings, Nativity sets in olive wood, olive wood and mother-of-pearl bound Bibles, and reproductions of antiquities are the souvenirs usually purchased by Christian visitors. The Baptist Book Store in East Jerusalem, on Rasheed Street, about two blocks from Herod's Gate, offers quality items at below average prices.

The visitor to Israel is offered several different opportunities to tour the country. This guidebook was developed as the Syllabus of Study for an annual Bibleland Seminar that the author has conducted for many

The author stands beside a rotary millstone excavated at Capernaum.

years. Assisted by a faculty of seminary and college professors, on the spot lectures, inspirational services and evening seminars are conducted in conjunction with the daily program of travel and sightseeing. Pastors, Sunday School teachers, and Bible students who want inspiration and instruction beyond the ordinary sightseeing tour may secure details from Bible-Land Travel, Box 5, Louisville, Kentucky 40201.

Practically all Christian tourists to Israel go in organized tour groups. There is considerable savings in the group airfare as well as in ground arrangements. (For example, the cheapest tourist air ticket from New York to Tel Aviv costs more than the total price of the average group tour which includes the reduced group airfare, hotels, meals, transportation, sightseeing, guides, etc.) Wholesale Tours International, 387 Park Avenue, North, New York, New York 10016, offers a number of itineraries for group travel.

The knowledgeable independent traveler has no difficulty touring Israel although it is generally more expensive than group travel. Buses operate throughout the country. Taxis are available in the cities, and limousines with a driver-guide can be hired. You-drive-it cars are also available. An international driver's license is required. A list of hotels, eating places, kibbutz guest houses, and Christian hospices along with road maps and other touring information may be secured from the Israel Government Tourist Office, 5 South Wabash Avenue, Suite 1402, Chicago, Illinois 60603.

The author gathered with a seminar group on the Mount of Olives—Jerusalem in the background

Excavations along the western wall of the Temple area in Jerusalem

Ancient baptismal pools at Qumran

Ruins of a synogogue at Capernaum

The scriptorium discovered at Qumran

Our Lord knelt "'neath the old olive trees" in the Garden of Gethsemane.